Natural Philosopher Trilogy

Meditations at Sunset

"The third and last volume of Trefil's 'Natural Philosopher' trilogy, and the best."
—*The New York Times Book Review*

Meditations at 10,000 Feet

"James Trefil has written a series of books that explain in a lucid and graceful way many of the branches of physics."
—*The New Yorker*

"The essays are lucidly written. . . . An impressive achievement in science writing for the general public."
—*The New York Times Book Review*

A Scientist at the Seashore

"It's so easy to understand yet so dense with knowledge that you'll never look at waves on a beach the same way again."
—*San Francisco Chronicle*

"A marvelous excursion from the beach to the ends of the solar system, an excursion at once scientifically accurate and stylistically captivating."
—*The New York Times Book Review*

"An ingenious and well-written book."
—*Washington Post Book World*

Meditations at Sunset

A Scientist Looks at the Sky

by James Trefil

Illustrations by Judith Peatross

COLLIER BOOKS
Macmillan Publishing Company
New York

Collier Books
Macmillan Publishing Company
866 Third Avenue, New York, NY 10022
Collier Macmillan Canada, Inc.

Library of Congress Cataloging-in-Publication Data
Trefil, James S., 1938–
Meditations at sunset : a scientist looks at the sky / by James Trefil;
illustrations by Judith Peatross. —1st Collier Books ed.
p. cm.
Includes index.
ISBN 0-02-025760-0
1. Meteorology—Popular works.   I. Title.
QC863.4.T74   1988
551.5—dc19   87-36745
                                                         CIP

First Collier Books Edition 1988

Macmillan books are available at special discounts for bulk
purchases for sales promotions, premiums, fund-raising, or
educational use. For details, contact:
Special Sales Director
Macmillan Publishing Company
866 Third Avenue
New York, NY 10022

10 9 8 7 6 5 4 3 2 1

Printed in the United States of America

Contents

Contents

Author's Note

Preface

This is the third book in a series dedicated to illustrating a simple but very profound point: the laws of nature that scientists discover at great effort and expense in their laboratories can be seen working all around us in the natural world. You can learn about them in laboratories, of course, but you can also learn about them simply by looking at a sunset, a mountain range, or even a handful of sand. Sometimes, in fact, seeing the laws of the universe operating in nature is a much better way to gain an appreciation of the way the world works than by looking at an artificially contrived experiment.

A second message is equally simple and equally profound: it turns out that the number of laws of nature needed to describe the world is very small. There are three laws of mechanics, four of electricity and magnetism, three for thermodynamics, one for relativity, and a few more (depending on how you count) for quantum mechanics. This means that all of the billions of natural phenomena we encounter every day are comprehensible using only a few natural laws. The situation is analogous to a large web, with the phenomenon at the periphery and the laws at the center. You can enter the web at any point, but if you work your way back, you eventually come to one of the great principles of natural law. This explains why it is as easy to study the universe at a beach as in a laboratory. It also tells us that there must be many connections between phenomena that, on the surface, appear unrelated. This concept of a connected, interrelated universe governed by a small number of guiding principles is the crowning achievement of Western science.

In the two previous books in the "Natural Philosopher" series, *A Scientist at the Seashore* and *Meditations at 10,000 Feet*, I took as my point of departure a walk along the beach and a hike in the mountains. If it makes no difference where you start into the web, there's no reason not to pick someplace pleasant. Readers and reviewers were kind enough to express amazement that so much could be learned from such simple observations. The *Washington Post* even expressed mock horror at the excesses this approach might bring and asked if *The Physics of the Bedroom* was next on the list.

The only problem with the beaches and mountains is that for most people they are, like the laboratory, rather special places— places to visit on vacation but not really part of everyday experience. In this book, therefore, I have taken on the job of entering the web of knowledge at points we all share— observations of phenomena such as sunsets, clouds, and lightning bolts. There's as much physics in a good thunderstorm as in a synchrotron, and a lot more people have been around the former than the latter. The phenomena of the weather affect us all directly, as is illustrated in the effects of microbursts on commercial airliners (see chapter 6). They also lead to unexpected places, as is illustrated by the connection between the fact that you can't get a suntan through a window and the existence of quarks (see chapter 11).

The way that light comes through the atmosphere, the clouds and storms we see, and the colors of a sunset can be seen by anyone who is willing to look. Indeed, between the time I wrote chapter 14 and the time I wrote this preface, I saw ball lightning for the first time. It accompanied a lightning stroke that hit uncomfortably close to my car while I was driving through a storm on the plains of Wyoming. I can't guarantee you'll all see ball lightning or the green flash (see chapter 1), of course, but I can guarantee that if you absorb the lessons of this book, you'll look at things you see in the sky with new eyes. My profound hope is that the next time you fly in an airplane and look down at the clouds, you won't just see a lumpy layer of white but an entry point into the mysteries of the entire universe.

Meditations at Sunset

ONE

Meditations at Sunset

THE MOST SPECTACULAR SUNSET I ever saw was in New Jersey. Actually, the sunset was in New Jersey, but I wasn't. I was perched in a hotel room high above midtown Manhattan, looking southwest over the Jersey coast at the flat plains that hold one of the biggest concentrations of oil refineries in the world. It was a clear, windless winter day—perfect conditions for the formation of stable layers of various kinds of hydrocarbons in the atmosphere. As the sun sank toward the horizon, the light coming through this layered ooze began to do strange things. The sun appeared to grow corners, so that its rim looked like a curved staircase instead of a smooth disk. Each step marked the boundary of a different hydrocarbon layer running across the sun, and each layer was a slightly different shade of orange or red. As this banded apparition sank toward the horizon, it didn't so much set as dissolve into a filmy cloud.

I was attending a convention of physicists, and the next day I described what I had seen to a number of my friends. We were all assistant professors at the time, and the tonier restaurants of Manhattan were a bit out of our reach. We decided to stock up at a nearby delicatessen and have a picnic in my room to see if the sunset would repeat itself. If anything, it was better the second evening, though whether because of the company, the wine, or the atmosphere I will never know. And although I enjoyed the sunsets immensely, I have to admit that there was one sight I enjoyed even more: the expression on the desk clerk's face as we trooped through his ornate lobby with our brown-bag dinners.

The most striking thing about sunsets, of course, is the display of colors in the sky. The sun, which shines yellow all day, turns a brilliant orange or red as it sets, and this light, reflected from clouds, turns large areas of the sky the same color. It is probably the slowly changing and darkening colors that give the sunset its particularly calm and peaceful aura. But if someday you are watching a sunset and find yourself in a mood for something more than relaxed contemplation, you can learn a great deal about nature from the display.

For example, one obvious question you might ask is why the sun appears to change color when it nears the horizon. It's obvious that the sun itself can't change color in a matter of a few hours, and even if it could, it could hardly appear red to you and at the same time yellow to someone a few thousand miles to the west. Thus the change in color must have something to do with the earth's atmosphere.

While we're pondering the color of the sun at sunset, we could equally well ask why the sun appears to be yellow at noon. After all, we know from pictures taken by astronauts in space that the sun as seen from above the atmosphere appears to be pure white. The change in color from white in space to yellow on the ground must also have something to do with the passage of light through the atmosphere. As it turns out, one of those unexpected connections I discussed in the preface of this book is this: when we have figured out why sunsets are beautiful, we will also have explained why the sky is blue.*

---

*A detailed discussion of the mechanism of the blue sky is given in my book *The Unexpected Vista* (Scribners, 1983).

The clue to the appearance of the sun when seen through the blanket of the earth's atmosphere is that white light, the type emitted by the sun, is made up of a spectrum of all visible colors: red, orange, yellow, green, blue, and violet. Isaac Newton discovered this in the seventeenth century by passing sunlight through a glass prism and observing the colors spread out on a sheet of paper, then using another prism to recombine those colors to reproduce the original white light. You can see the same thing yourself when sunlight hits water droplets in a rain shower and produces a rainbow.

When a beam of light composed of all the colors in the spectrum strikes the top of the earth's atmosphere, it encounters atoms of oxygen, nitrogen, and other components of the air that can cause the beam to scatter. Think of the light as a continuous stream of marbles coming from the sun and the atmosphere as a thin layer of shifting, moving obstacles like bowling balls. In such a situation, most of the marbles will be able to penetrate some distance through the collection of obstacles, but some will hit those obstacles and be scattered out of the beam. In just that way, most of the light in the beam from the sun comes straight through to the surface of the earth without ever striking an atom, but some part of the beam will be lost through collisions.

It is a property of atoms that their ability to interact with light of any type and scatter it depends on the color of that light. Blue light, which has the highest energy of the visible spectrum, is scattered most intensely, while red light, the least energetic, is scattered most weakly. When sunlight enters the top of the atmosphere, it is an equal mixture of all colors, but as it progresses and is scattered by atoms, the energetic blue light begins to be winnowed out of the beam. By the time it reaches the surface of the earth, the light has gone from being a white beam to one that has been depleted in the blue end of the spectrum. The consequence: the predominant color of the beam is now yellow. This is why the sun appears to be yellow during the day.

As the scattering continues, more and more of the light from the blue end of the spectrum is removed. If this depletion went on long enough, only red light would be left. When the sun is overhead, its light comes down to us through several miles of atmosphere—enough to turn it yellow, yet not enough to remove everything but the red. But at sunset the sunlight skims horizontally along the surface of the earth. Hence the beam passes through a much greater thickness of atmosphere and undergoes more scattering as it does so. The sun is bound to appear red, as we know it does.

Thus far we have considered only the beam of light that comes to us directly from the sun. But what about the light that is removed from that beam by scattering? Imagine what happens and the connection between sunset and blue sky will become clear. When we look at the sky away from the sun, we are seeing light that has been scattered twice: once out of the direct beam, as described above, and once more by some atoms in the atmosphere that direct it toward our eyes. Since blue is much more likely to be scattered than other colors, the light that reaches our eye from regions of the sky away from the sun is blue. What we are seeing is light that has been scattered by the atmosphere, first away from the sun and then toward our eyes.

The sun is yellow during the day—why? Because blue light has been removed from the beam by scattering. The sky is blue—why? Because we are seeing the scattered light. The sun is red at sunset—why? Because even more scattering has occurred. All these phenomena are connected through the laws that govern the interaction of light with atoms.

This explanation of the color of the sky was first proposed by John Tyndall, a nineteenth-century Anglo-Irish scientist. He is known to modern physicists as the discoverer of the "Tyndall effect." This is what occurs when a beam of light travels through air that carries small particles such as smoke or dust in suspension. Light scatters from these particles and comes to your eye, allowing you to see the beam. Something of a laboratory curiosity in Tyndall's time, this effect has become very useful to people who work with lasers. Lasers emit very tight beams of light, and in clean air there is so little scattering that often you can hardly see the beam unless it shines directly onto a surface. If you put some particles in the air (e.g., by clapping some blackboard erasers nearby), then laser light will scatter from the beam to your eye; you can then see it and are able to point it in the direction you want it to go. The chances are that pictures you have seen of lasers, pictures showing beams of light bouncing around in mirrors and the like, were taken just after dust had been put into the air to make the beam visible.

Tyndall, by the way, was a most interesting person. In addition to studying the nature of light, he was a major popularizer and teacher of science. A leader in the British educational movement, he gave lectures to overflow crowds of factory workers in cities all over England. His scientific curiosity was wide. He was, for example, an early supporter of Louis Pasteur's germ theory of disease, and it was Tyndall's experiments that showed once and for all that life did not arise by spontaneous generation. Before his work, a sizable body of scientific opinion held that life arose spontaneously in decaying organisms—maggots, for example, were thought to have been created spontaneously in the bodies of dead animals. Tyndall demolished this old chestnut by keeping carcasses in sterile conditions and observing that no life developed. Finally, in his later years he spent summers in the Alps and did pioneering work on the flow of glaciers; no doubt he enjoyed the sunsets there.

There is, of course, more to a good sunset than just the redness of the sun. A really good display requires enough clouds to reflect the red light but not so many that the sun itself is obscured. A perfect sunset is a thing to savor. In Japan, I have been told, there is a special tea ceremony to be performed while watching the sunset. In Key West, Florida, people go down to the docks to watch the sun go down. A particularly good show gets a round of applause.

But even in sunsets that are less than perfect there are all sorts of interesting things going on. For example, you may have noticed that as the sun approaches the horizon, it appears to flatten out; its shape becomes more elliptical than circular, another example of the way the passage of light through the atmosphere can affect the appearance of the sun. The apparent flattening results from the familiar effect known as refraction.

When a beam of light passes from one material to another, it changes direction. A few examples of this effect are shown in

Figure 1.1, below. When you see a friend standing up in a swimming pool as on the left, it often appears that your friend's legs are somehow out of proportion—they look shorter than they should. The reason is that a beam of light reflected from your friend's foot travels to your eye along the bent path shown. As you see things, your friend's foot is located in the direction from which the light enters your eye;

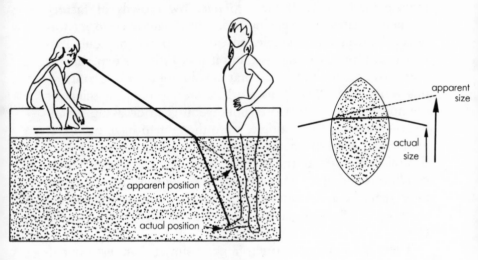

FIGURE 1.1

hence you see it along the dotted line in the figure. Because water is denser than air, the light beam was bent at the surface of the water, so that the dotted line lies above the actual path of the light in water. Your friend's feet therefore appear closer to her waist than they actually are. A similar effect makes an object appear larger when viewed through a glass lens, as shown on the right.

Similarly, the material of the atmosphere is not of constant density: it varies from place to place, depending on altitude and temperature. You know, for example, that air gets thinner as you climb a mountain—that is why distance runners raised in a high-altitude environment do so well in events such as the marathon, in which the lungs must use oxygen with maximum efficiency. In effect, light passing through air is undergoing a continuous transition from one density to another; consequently, light beams from objects such as the sun follow curved paths, as shown in Figure 1.2, below.

A number of consequences follow from the occurrence of refraction in the atmosphere. For one thing, it is entirely possible that when you are looking at a sunset, the sun might be actually *below* the horizon. You can still see the sun, however, because the atmosphere refracts the light, bends it "around the corner" and into your eyes. Refraction makes the sun appear higher in the sky than it actually is.

The flattened appearance of the sun is also a consequence of refraction. Light coming from the bottom edge of the sun has to travel through a slightly thicker layer of air than light coming from the top edge. Both beams undergo refraction, of course, but the one from the bottom edge is refracted farther from its original path. This moves the perceived upper edge of the sun above its actual position, and it moves the perceived lower edge even higher up. The net effect is to make the face of the sun seem shorter in the vertical direction than in the horizontal. This causes the "flattening" of the sun near the

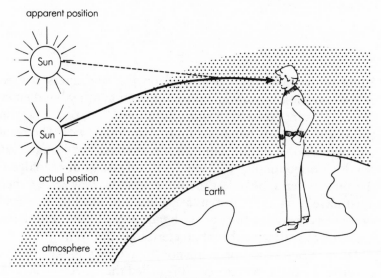

FIGURE 1.2

horizon. (It doesn't occur when the sun is directly overhead, because then light from the top and bottom edges traverses roughly equal amounts of atmosphere.)

The "corners" that I saw on the sun in the New Jersey sunset were also caused by refraction. The atmosphere through which the light passed consisted of a series of relatively stable layers of air, each differing significantly in density from the one above it. The amount of refraction incurred by the light coming through each layer was different, and hence the apparent position of the band across the sun that gave rise to that light would be shifted by a different amount. You can see what this does to the appearance of the sun by consulting Figure 1.3.

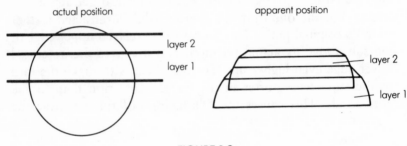

FIGURE 1.3

Suppose the light from one band on the sun enters one so-called inversion layer, while the light from another band enters the next layer. Refraction shifts both bands up, of course, but suppose that it lifts band one more than band two. The result will be as shown on the right. At the interface between the two bands, a discontinuity or "step" will be visible at the edge of the sun. When I looked at the sun setting in New Jersey, there must have been half a dozen layers, each producing the steps I saw. The different colors of the bands arose from the different amounts of scattering that characterized each layer.

There is one sunset phenomenon I have long looked for but never seen except in pictures. It is called the "green flash." As the last bit of the sun disappears below the horizon, if the conditions are just right, you are supposed to see a flash of pure green light. According to an old legend from the Highlands of Scotland, written down by the French novelist Jules Verne, "At its appearance all deceit and falsehood are done away, and he who has been fortunate enough to behold it is enabled to see closely into his own heart and to read the thoughts of others."

In the nineteenth century a number of explanations for the green flash were advanced, including one that stated that it was an illusion created by disorders of the liver. There is no need to suffer such an affliction to see and understand the green flash; it arises from a combination of the effects of scattering and refraction already discussed. Light beams bend when they encounter new materials, and the amount of bending depends on the color of the light. In general, blue light bends less than red. It is this property that allowed Newton to separate out the colors in sunlight by passing it through a prism. It is this same property that gives rise to the colors of the rainbow.

As the sun sinks below the horizon, the rays are bent as shown in Figure 1.4, the blue rays being bent a bit less than the red. You might therefore expect that the last color to be seen would be blue. But we must remember that this last bit of sunlight is coming through the air, where the blue light is being scattered out of the beam. It turns out that the last color of

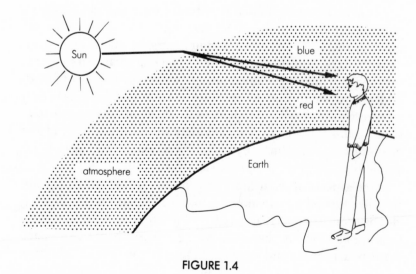

FIGURE 1.4

light to get through the atmosphere with enough intensity to remain unscattered—and hence visible—is green. Thus we see—if we're lucky—a green and not a blue flash.

I could go on discussing various peculiar sunset effects for a long time, but all of them, like the green flash, can be understood through the way that light interacts with atoms in the atmosphere. But hold on a minute! We can turn this process around. We can deduce the properties and composition of the atmosphere by seeing what happens to light as it passes through it.

For example, that the sun appears red at sunset tells us that blue light is scattered from the constituents of the atmosphere more readily than red. If the atmosphere were composed of relatively large particles, such as smoke, this would not be true: all colors of light would be scattered about equally. From this we conclude that the appearance of the sunset indicates an atmosphere made up of particles much smaller than the wavelength of light—particles roughly the size of atoms and molecules. We could draw this conclusion even if we were unable to get our hands on samples of the atmosphere and isolate the atoms in our laboratory.

This insight may not seem especially wonderful when our concern is with the earth's atmosphere. We can, after all, obtain samples of it for routine analysis. But in the universe at large there are many materials whose properties can be ascertained only through the effect they have on light that passes through them. To give one example among many, light from distant stars comes to us after traveling many light-years through the interstellar medium. If we are to use this light to understand the objects from which it emanates, we must form a correct idea of what happens to it on its journey to our telescopes; and this, in turn, means that we must understand the medium through which it passes. Here, obviously, there is no possibility of getting samples to analyze.

Some aspects of what lies between stars is familiar to anyone who has looked at astronomy books. There are huge, glowing clouds of gasses and regions of cool gas that emit radio waves. Less well known is that even in the darkest regions of space there is a thin shroud of dust. This dust makes up about 1 percent of the total mass of the interstellar material. Its presence was first detected by the analysis of light from distant stars.

I hasten to add that the presence of dust does not contradict the common idea that the interstellar medium is a vacuum—it is. The concentration of dust is tiny—about one dust particle in a volume the size of a typical skyscraper. Moreover, interstellar dust is not made from the kind of dust you vacuum up from your floor. The individual grains are the size of a few hundred or perhaps a few thousand atoms on a side—much too small to be seen with the unaided eye. Yet though the size of the grains is small and they are widely scattered in space, the light that travels through them for hundreds of light-years is affected, just as surely as it is affected by coming a shorter distance through the denser atmosphere of the earth.

The first intimation that there might be a hitherto unseen interstellar medium came in the 1930s from astronomers at Lick Observatory in California. They were measuring the size of large clusters of stars in the Milky Way, using the technique sketched in Figure 1.5. First they would measure the angle between the top and the bottom of the cluster in the sky, and then, by comparing the amount of light reaching us from stars in the cluster with the amount of light emitted by the same type of star close to the earth, they estimated the distance to the cluster, *D*. Once we have *D*, simple geometry yields the size of the cluster.

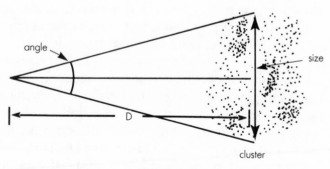

FIGURE 1.5

When the stargazers at Lick carried out the measurements, they obtained a seemingly paradoxical result. The farther away from the earth a cluster was, the larger it seemed to be. This result was hard to accept for two reasons. In the first place, there is no reason why the size of star clusters should depend on where they are in the sky. In the second, that the size of clusters depends on distance from the earth seemed to imply that the earth occupies a privileged place in the great scheme of things. This conclusion flies in the face of one of the major tenets of modern astronomy. Ever since Copernicus, any hint that the earth might occupy a special place in the universe has been viewed with extreme disapproval by scientists. Consequently, the data obtained on the size of star clusters were regarded with a good deal of skepticism. In the time-honored tradition of scientists confronted with results that seem to lead in undesirable directions, astronomers began looking for alternative explanations of the facts. Had it turned out that no such explanations could be found, they would of course have had to rethink the Copernican axiom. Fortunately, a way out presented itself quickly.

Suppose, they argued, that interstellar space was filled with tiny dust particles. A light beam traveling through a dusty medium will grow dimmer and dimmer as the light is scattered from the beam. This means that a star in a distant cluster will appear to be dimmer than it would be if there were no intervening dust. In the original analysis, this dimness was falsely attributed to a great distance between the earth and the star. If you think the cluster is much farther away than it actually is, you will think that its true size is larger than its actual size, as well. Interstellar dust provided a neat explanation of the result that astronomers did not want to take at face value.

If this were the end of the story, it would not constitute a very edifying tale about the methods of modern science. It would appear that astronomers had rescued Copernicus by making up an explanation out of whole cloth, without any evidence that the dust was really there. But once the idea of interstellar dust was proposed, a number of observations were made to confirm or refute its existence and—if present—to determine its composition. This last problem—finding out what the dust is made of—remains a major research topic today.

Our analysis of the sunset suggests one way that dust might affect light from distant stars. If the particles are not too large, they ought to scatter more blue light than red, that is, there ought to be a reddening of the beam. This reddening is now routinely measured in astronomical observations. There are also other, somewhat more subtle effects of interstellar dust on light as it passes between its source and the earth. By analyzing how light is absorbed and changed as it passes through the dust grains, we can form some idea of the dust's composition.

Although the existence of interstellar dust was suggested (and confirmed) by observing its effect on transmitted light, our most direct knowledge of it comes from modern measurements of radiation emitted by the dust itself. As a dust grain sits in space, it absorbs light from the stars and slowly heats up. Then, like a coal in a fireplace, it begins to give off infrared radiation—radiation that we cannot detect with the eye but which can easily be measured with instruments.

The net result of all of the data on interstellar dust is a somewhat sketchy, not to say messy, picture of what lies out there between the stars. One thing is clear: in our galaxy, there is not one single kind of dust particle. It is impossible to explain the effects that dust has on light unless we posit a rather wide range of grain size and composition. We assume a distribution of grains whose sizes range from about fifty to two thousand atoms on a side—small by earthly standards. The best guess is that these grains are as sketched in Figure 1.6, with a core of some solid material like silicon or carbon, surrounded by a layer of ice. This ice may be ordinary water ice, but it could be dry ice (solid carbon dioxide) or even ice made from methane or ammonia. Scattering from an assortment of such grains could explain both the dimming and the reddening of light that is observed. Thus, just as observing light in the atmosphere at sunset would, in principle, allow us to determine something about the composition of the atmosphere, observing light coming through the interstellar space has allowed us to determine the composition of the rarefied matter that exists there.

Before leaving this subject, we should note a few more points

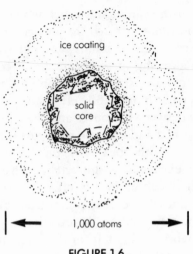

FIGURE 1.6

about the effects on light of the interstellar medium and of the atmosphere. Although we have concentrated our attention on those situations in which the light is affected by the medium through which it passes, it is clear that most of the light in both cases simply comes through unaffected. You can convince yourself of this in our atmosphere by noting that the brightness of a star or planet does not change perceptibly as it moves from the zenith to the horizon, even though the amount of atmosphere it traverses during this interval changes by a factor of ten or more. If changing the thickness of air by so much does not alter the amount of light sufficiently to be detected by the eye, then air cannot by itself absorb or scatter much light. And if this is true for the atmosphere, it must be even truer for the much more rarefied interstellar medium; for the light that reaches us from the most distant reaches of the universe passes through more material in the first mile of the atmosphere than the total it has encountered in space. Still, though the interstellar medium and our atmosphere differ widely in kind and density, it's comforting to know that they can both be described by the same laws of nature and that each is capable of producing its own brand of sunset.

TWO

Of Clocks and Calendars

S UNSET MARKS THE END of the day. This is a simple, almost trivial statement, and yet the idea that time can be divided into repeatable units like the day is a very profound one. Even our most primitive civilizations must have some notion of time and some way of marking its passage, if only to keep track of religious festivals. The day—the length of time between one sunset and the next—is a natural way to measure time. So is the year, which measures the time it takes to go through the cycle of the seasons.

Here let me make a general philosophical point before going further. I am going to be talking about "time" in this chapter, but I want to avoid getting bogged down in unanswerable questions such as "What is time?" The best answer I've ever heard to this question was in a comedy skit at the Second City, an improvisational theater group in Chicago.

The speaker, in a pseudo-Germanic accent, was giving a lecture on "Ze Universe." At one point he asked "Vat is this thing called time?" He then paused. The pause lengthened. Then, just as you were starting to wonder whether something was wrong, he said, "Zat was time!" From my point of view, this remains the best answer to the general philosophical problem posed by the questions—at least I've never seen anyone do better.

For all its indefinability, time is really no different from other physical quantities like weight, length, and temperature. We do not define any of these in the abstract. Instead, we arbitrarily define a basic unit of weight or length or whatever and then refer all other measurements to that basic unit. For example, the question "What is weight?"* or "What is length?" is just as unanswerable as the question "What is time?" But somehow weight and length don't seem to carry the emotional charge that time does, so this similarity often goes unremarked.

With no need to define length in the abstract, however, we yet feel the need for a standard unit of length—the meter or the foot. At one time the meter was defined as the distance between two scratches on a platinum-iridium bar kept in a vault at the International Bureau of Weights and Measures near Paris. It is now defined in terms of the properties of atoms (about which I shall say more later). Weight is still defined in terms of the properties of a block of platinum-iridium alloy kept at that same institution. All other lengths and weights are assigned numbers by comparing them to these standards. We can thus proceed with the practical everyday business of quantifying distances and weights without ever having to tackle the vexing problem of what distance or weight *is*.

I suspect that the failure to say what time is bothers people because time seems to touch us intimately—we feel its passage, we are aware of aging, of events being irretrievably gone—and the simple act of quantifying time does not meet

---

*The expert will notice that I am being a little casual here in speaking of weight instead of mass. The reader who minds is invited to substitute mass for weight when it appears in the text.

the deep-seated need to cope with these feelings. Nevertheless, from the restricted point of view of the physicist, time is
no different from any other fundamental quantity.

If we want to think about time scientifically, it is clear that
we have to find some basic unit by which to measure it.
Today we use the second as this unit, but the use of such a
short period of time is possible only in a relatively advanced
civilization, one capable of building clocks. The day and the
year are easier to measure without clocks and were therefore
the units of time of early civilizations. The general plan is
this: first, find some regularly recurring process. This may be
the swing of a pendulum, the vibration of a quartz crystal,
the rotation of the earth on its axis, the motion of the earth
around the sun, or the motion of an electron in an atom.
The unit of time—second, day, year—is defined in terms of
the basic process.

The earliest task faced by those concerned with marking
the passage of time was the construction of a calendar. A
calendar is a device that relates two basic units of time—the
time it takes the earth to complete one orbit around the sun
and the time it takes the earth to complete one revolution on
its axis. The need for such a device is obvious in any agri-
cultural society. The season and the weather are determined
by the position of the earth in its orbit, but the easiest unit
of time to count is the day. Therefore, if the earth is at the
right place for the planting of seeds today, the calendar tells
us how many days to count until we ought to plant our
seeds next year. But the task of constructing a calendar is
made difficult by the fact that the length of the year is not
an exact number of days.

The first calendar was developed by the Egyptians. It contained twelve months of thirty days each, for a total of 360,
and then a five-day holiday. Our New Year's celebrations are
thought to descend from the year-end revels of the Egyptians. While this Egyptian calendar is better than none, it
has a serious flaw. It assumes a year of 365 days, while the
actual year is roughly 365¼ days. In such a calendar, the
position of the earth next New Year's Day will be about six
hours farther back along the orbit than it is now; the year

after that it will be back twelve hours, and so on. Thus, the Egyptian calendar gets out of synchronization with the seasons pretty quickly. Indeed, the position of the earth on "New Year's Day" will go all the way around the orbit in a period of 1,460 years. This was perceived by the Egyptians, and in 123 B.C. the rulers of Alexandria decided to insert an extra day every four years, thereby introducing a correction like our own leap year. The decree wasn't enforced vigorously, however, and normal human cussedness guaranteed that the old system, where virtually every city had its own calendar, remained in effect for a good while.

It was Julius Caesar who, dismayed at the inconvenience of running an empire in which people could not even agree on the date, instituted the first worldwide calendar reform. In order to get things back to where they should be, he inserted two extra months plus twenty-three extra days for February into 46 B.C. This was the longest year on record, totaling 455 days. After this, the Julian calendar inserted a leap day every four years. We get most of the names of the months (including July for Julius Caesar) from this calendar. Originally, New Year's Day was March 1, which explains the names of September, October, November, and December (which use the Latin roots for seven to ten).

Unfortunately, the true year is not exactly 365¼ days either; it is eleven minutes, fourteen seconds shorter. As soon as Caesar promulgated the Julian calendar, this error started to accumulate. It amounted to roughly seven days in every thousand years. By 1545, the vernal equinox (which church fathers used to set the date for Easter) had drifted ten days, and the Council of Trent authorized the pope to straighten things out. Accordingly, in 1582, Pope Gregory XIII issued orders for a new calendar. To get the equinox back to March 21, he ordered that the day after October 5 would be October 15. The year 1582, in other words, was the shortest year on record, lacking nine days. From that point on, leap years occurring in centennial years would be observed only once every four hundred years. Thus, although 1700, 1800, and 1900 ought to have been leap years, they weren't. The year 2000, however, will be a leap year. The Gregorian calendar, as it is called, is what we use today.

In Russia, the Gregorian calendar was never adopted, and the errors in the Julian system continued to accumulate. When the Soviet Union abandoned the Julian calendar in 1918, a total of thirteen days were lost. This is why there is occasional confusion about whether the Russian Revolution was in October or November.

Once the calendar had been straightened out, attention turned to shorter divisions of time. The Egyptians were in the habit of dividing daylight into twelve equal periods—the analogue of our modern hours. But the Egyptians defined their hour as one-twelfth of the time between dawn and dusk, which meant that the actual length of the hour varied from one part of the year to the next. This system is well suited to measuring the passage of time with a sundial but leaves something to be desired at night.

It wasn't until well into the Middle Ages that better ways of marking time came into common use. It always comes as a surprise to many people to discover that some great technological advance was made during the "Dark Ages." The fact is that the period before the Renaissance saw the introduction of many important devices. The windmill, the printing press, and the compass (borrowed from China) were only a few of the more visible advances. The use of algebra also had its beginnings then. I suspect that the view of the Middle Ages taught in our schools is strongly influenced by the lack of progress in basic science during that period. We are taught that the scientists of the day were absorbed by the imaginary debate as to "how many angels can dance on the head of a pin" rather than by divining the tenets of basic science, and we ignore the fact that outside the universities men with little education but clever hands were slowly developing the tools and machines that would serve as the basis for the coming explosion of technology.

Indeed it appears that the main driving force for the development of the mechanical clock was the foundation of the Benedictine order in the fifth century. St. Benedict specified that monks in his order were to perform certain religious devotions at 9:00 P.M., midnight, and 3:00 A.M. (as well as at various times during the day). This meant that at least one brother had to stay awake to watch a candle burn down so that he could wake everyone at the appointed hours. For that lonely monk, the motivation to find a better way to measure time must have been pretty strong. We know from indirect evidence that by the twelfth century some sort of clock run by dripping water was in use. We know this because in 1198 a monk called Jocelyn de Brakelund put down an account of a great fire in the monastery at Bury St. Edmonds in England. He wrote that when the fire was discovered, "the young men among us ran to get water, some to the well and others *to the clock*." By the fourteenth century, the water clock (which probably froze during the winter months) had been replaced by the familiar mechanical clock. Cities vied with each other for the honor of having the most beautiful and elaborate clock tower. One group of businessmen in the town of Lyons in France petitioned the town council to build a clock tower because "if such a clock were to be made, more merchants would come to our fairs, the citizens would be consoled, cheerful, and happy, and would lead a more orderly life. . . . " Apparently, overselling projects to the government is not a practice that began with us moderns.

Once the use of clocks was widespread, the need arose for synchronization—for the establishment of a common time. The obvious period to use was the length of the day, since the rotation of the earth seemed to be the sort of steady, repeating motion needed to define a basic unit. By international agreement, the second was defined to be 1/86,400 of the mean solar day. (For our purposes, you can think of the mean solar day as the average time between successive passages of the sun through a point directly overhead—in effect, the time from one noon to the next.*)

This definition of the basic unit of time, which uses the rotation of the earth as the repeating process in terms of which all other times are measured, was good enough to last well into the twentieth century. The rotation of the earth is, indeed, regular, provided you don't examine it too closely. One day is very nearly as long as another, so defining the

*The detailed definition of the second is actually a bit complicated, because the motion of the sun across the sky is not uniform from one day to the next, a fact that reflects the elliptical shape of the earth's orbit and the speeding up of the earth when it is closest to the sun.

second as a certain fraction of a day worked quite well.

Of course, this statement was true only so long as other methods of determining time were insufficiently accurate to detect irregularities in the rotation time. To see why this is so, imagine yourself living back in the heyday of the pharoahs. If you had no clocks other than a sundial, the difference in length between the "hour" at different times of the year would mean very little to you. If you had another type of clock, however, even a cheap modern wristwatch, you would quickly see that the unit of time defined by the sundial wasn't keeping in line with your mechanical timekeeper. You would not need a particularly accurate watch to make this discovery—a machine that kept time to within a few minutes would do.

In the same way, when very accurate pendulum clocks (which are nothing more than sophisticated versions of the familiar grandfather clock) began to be developed at the end of the nineteenth century, it quickly became apparent that various processes that affect the rotation of the earth also affect the length of the second. These effects are small; today we know that the most accurate clocks gain about one second per year when compared to the year defined in terms of solar time. Nevertheless, as the demand for increasingly accurate standards of time grew, it became clear that the solid earth is actually a fairly jittery body and that units based on its rotation would not do for modern technology.

The reasons for the earth's shaky rotation are many. The easiest to understand is the effect of the tides. We know that the moon raises tides twice daily in the earth's oceans. These tides, together with analogous effects on the solid earth itself, have the effect of slowing down its rotation and lengthening the day. We can see this effect dramatically rendered by looking at the daily growth rings in fossil coral beds. These rings (which are like the yearly growth rings on trees) show that four hundred million years ago the length of the day was between twenty-one and twenty-two hours, as opposed to the present twenty-four.* Our best present estimate is that

---

*A detailed discussion of the way that tides affect the earth and the moon is given in my book *Scientist at the Seashore* (Scribners, 1984).

the tides are causing the length of the day to increase by about 2 milliseconds per century. Thus, January 1, 1987, was 2 milliseconds longer than January 1, 1887, and the twentieth century will be about a minute longer than the nineteenth.

While the effects of the tides are easy to visualize, they do not produce the largest variations in the length of the day. Those changes are caused by changes in the direction of the earth's axis of rotation.

To understand why a change in the direction of the earth's axis, though not in its rate of spin, can cause a change in the length of the day, look at Figure 2.1. If the earth is rotating with its axis vertical, as shown on the top, then the length of the day is defined in terms of the time it takes the sun to complete successive crossings of the meridian following the path shown. Now suppose that during the night the earth's axis suddenly shifts to the position shown below. Then the sun has to travel an extra distance to get to the new (slanted) meridian, and it will take longer to get there as measured by a clock on the ground. This lengthening of the day arises from the fact that the day is defined in terms of the sun crossing the meridian as seen by an observer at a fixed point on the surface of the earth. The shift of axis changes the position of that observer, thereby changing the length of the day even though the earth's spin has not slowed down.

This exaggerated example can be used to discuss the state of affairs on the real earth. The axis of the earth is undergoing a number of continuous changes of direction. The largest of these changes are quite well understood and were known to Greek and Babylonian astronomers. They result from the effects of the gravitational pull of the moon and other planets on the earth. One of these motions of the axis can be seen quite easily in the homely example of a child's top. The top spins rapidly on its axis, but the axis itself traces out a cone in space. The slow motion of the axis is called precession.

The axis of the earth undergoes precession, tracing out a full circle every 26,000 years. The change in the length of

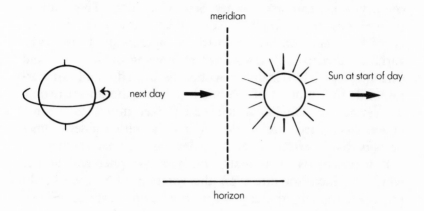

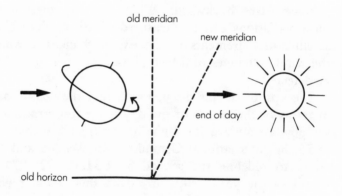

FIGURE 2.1

the day due to this effect was easily detected by the pendulum clocks used in the early twentieth century.

In addition to precession, the axis of the earth undergoes a small rocking motion called nutation. The effects of this motion on the length of the day was marginally discernible in the nineteenth century.

Finally, the axis of the earth undergoes an erratic motion known as the Chandler wobble, named after the nineteenth-century American astronomer Seth Chandler. This motion corresponds to a small precessionlike motion of the axis every fourteen months, on which is superimposed an erratic variation due to such things as the blowing of the wind and earthquakes. The Chandler wobble is indeed small—it corresponds to a motion of the north pole around an area some 40 feet across. Obviously, it need be taken into account only in extremely accurate work. It is only with modern timekeepers that its effect on the solar day has been determined.

It may surprise you that something as ephemeral as the wind can have an effect on the rotation of the earth. In principle, though, the statement should not surprise. When the wind starts to blow to the west, the earth should recoil to the east exactly as a rocket moves forward by kicking exhaust gases backward. What is truly surprising is that these variations can be measured. With modern clocks and satellite measurements of the earth, changes attributable to the wind—changes of a few milliseconds per day—can easily be detected.

The upshot of this discussion is that the second as defined in terms of the length of the day is far too erratic a thing to serve as a standard for "time in our time." Consequently, in 1956 the International Committee on Weights and Measures voted to redefine the second as $1/31,566,925.9747$ of the length of the year 1900. In effect, this action replaced the rotation of the earth by the movement of the earth around the sun as the regular phenomenon in terms of which we define the basic unit of time. The definition was given by reference to a particular year, because, like the length of the day, the length of each year changes by amounts large enough to be detected. Even as these deliberations were going on, however, discoveries were taking place through the study of the atom that would forever remove astronomical motion from its role as the determiner of time. I refer to the development of the atomic clock.

The essential feature of the atomic clock is that it replaces the erratic motion of the earth by the much more regular and precise motion of electrons in orbit around the nucleus of an atom. As a bit of doggerel in the physics folklore has it,

The pendulum's swing
is a variable thing,
so the atom's vibrating
has the highest rating.

To understand how the movement of an electron can be used to make the world's most accurate clock, we have to digress for a moment to go over some of the characteristics of the subatomic world. We all know that the atom consists of negatively charged electrons in orbit around a positively charged nucleus. Another, less well known property is that both electrons and nuclei can be thought of as tiny magnets, each with a north and a south pole. It is a property of magnets that they exert force on each other, with like poles repelling and unlike poles attracting. One result of this fact is that if two magnets lie near each other and one is moved, the other moves, as well. The motion of the second magnet, in turn, causes the first to move again, and this sort of thing goes on until friction dissipates all the energy and the magnets come to rest.

In an atom there is no friction—no winds blow on the electron. Consequently, the interplay of the magnets can go on forever. The result is as shown in Figure 2.2 below. The interaction between the nuclear and electron magnets causes both to undergo precession—the axis of rotation of each traces out a cone in space, just as the earth's axis does. But unlike the earth's precession there are few effects in the atom that can alter this precession. The time it takes for the axis of rotation of the electron's magnet to complete one cycle is the "tick" of the atomic clock.

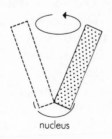
nucleus

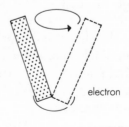
electron

FIGURE 2.2

In Figure 2.3 we illustrate another fact of subatomic magnetism—a fact that allows us to turn the regular precession of the electron into a practical timepiece. The nuclear magnets can be arranged in two ways—with the north poles pointing in the same direction or with the poles pointing in opposite directions. These two states of the electron have different energies, since the push on the electron has to be stronger to align its north pole with the north pole of the nucleus than it is for the opposite result. According to the laws of electromagnetism, if the atom is placed in a region flooded with radiation of the right frequency, it can absorb energy from the radiation and flip the electron from one orientation to another.

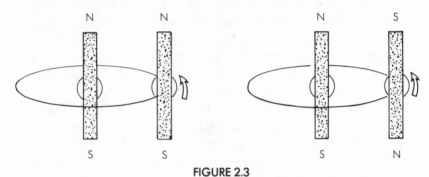

FIGURE 2.3

The working principle of the atomic clock is shown in Figure 2.4 (p. 29). For various technical reasons, the material used as a time standard is cesium, a silvery metal that is liquid at room temperatures. Cesium is heated in a small furnace until the atoms start to boil off. The atoms pass through a small slit in the furnace and move down a tube from which air has been removed. The temperature and the size of the slit are adjusted so that the atoms move down the tube in single file, not colliding with each other. The beam of cesium atoms first passes between the poles of a large magnet. The effect of this passage is to split the beam in two—atoms with their north poles pointing down go one direction; those with their north poles pointing up go the other. One of these beams then passes into a metal chamber into which precisely controlled microwave radiation is fed.

You can think of this chamber as a sort of high-tech micro-wave oven. If the frequency of the radiation is exactly right, it will cause the electron magnets to flip over in the atoms. The reversed beam is then passed through another magnet identical with the first. This magnet again divides the beam, separating those atoms with the electronic north poles in opposite directions. This second magnet is so adjusted that an atom that passes through the first magnet and then has its spin flipped will be directed to a detector, as shown.

The operation of the clock is simple. The beam is turned on, and the frequency of the microwave radiation is adjusted so that the maximum number of cesium atoms reaches the

THE ATOMIC CLOCK

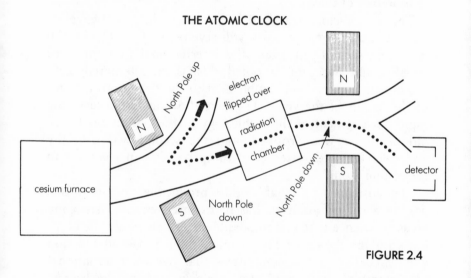

FIGURE 2.4

detector. When this is done, you know that the radiation is precisely tuned to the energy difference between the two states of the cesium atom. And since one cesium atom is exactly the same as any other cesium atom in the universe, every atomic clock must operate on exactly the same frequency as any other.

The atomic clock, then, gives us a way of producing microwaves with frequencies that can be reproduced to incredible levels of accuracy. The last time I looked, these frequencies were accurate to better than one part in a trillion. (That is to say, when the frequency is written down, the first uncertainty will occur in the twelfth digit!) This, in turn, means that such a clock can be used to define a time standard. To equate frequency with time, think about a familiar frequency, like the 60-cycles-per-second electrical current that runs all of your electrical appliances. The term "60 cycles" (or, to use the modern terminology, 60 hertz) means that the electrical current changes direction 120 times each second. If the reversals of electrical current were known very accurately, we could imagine defining the second as the time it takes for the current to reverse itself sixty times. This, too, would be a perfectly good time standard, one unrelated to the rotation of the earth.

The atomic-clock standard is the same: the microwave radiation in a fully tuned clock will reverse itself 9,192,631,770 times per second. In 1964, the International Committee of Weights and Measures adopted this as an alternative definition of the second—a supplement to the definition in terms of the length of the year. Then, in 1967, in response to the rapid development of the technology of the cesium clock, the old definition was dropped, and the second was officially and solely defined in terms of the precession of electrons in the cesium atom.

The existence of a reliable and reproducible clock with one part in a trillion accuracy has had consequences in so many areas of science that it is impossible to list them all. In keeping with the theme of this chapter, though, I shall mention one. Since 1972, the committees that oversee international time standards have used atomic clocks to keep the lengths of the day and year correct. The mechanism they use is simple. There are several standard clocks kept at laboratories around the earth. When a majority of these clocks show that the time defined by the rotation of the earth (called universal time, or UT) has gotten more than half a second out of line with the time being kept by cesium clocks, a decree goes out from the International Time Bureau. On a given day, at midnight, a "leap second" is inserted into all clocks running on UT. Thus is the turning of the earth kept synchronized with the atom.

THREE

Spots on the Sun

T HE STOCK MARKET seems to exert a fatal fascination on
some people—people who would never imagine that
they could win at roulette but who like to take a flyer
on the Big Board now and then. This little weakness is not
confined to our era. In the eighteenth century, for example, the
great Anglo-German astronomer Sir William Herschel made a
(reasonably successful) attempt to correlate the price of grain
in London with the appearance of sunspots. This wasn't a particularly quixotic idea. He reasoned that when there were a
large number of spots on the sun, it would give off less heat
and therefore cause bad weather on earth. This, in turn, would
affect the harvest, and hence the price of grain. He followed
the prices and sunspots for a few years and announced that he
found them to be correlated as he had predicted. Whether or
not he actually tried to put this knowledge to use by investing

in grain futures is not on record. I hope he didn't, because if he had, he would have lost his shirt.

During the late nineteenth and early twentieth centuries a large number of scientists lost their reputations, if not their shirts, following lines of investigations similar to Herschel's. Phenomena as diverse as the depth of Lake Michigan and the winter barometric pressure in northern India were claimed to be related to the appearance of spots on the sun, and an entire little industry grew up in the sciences based on these supposed correlations. When closer study and better data started to become available, however, the entire thing collapsed like a house of cards. It is only within the last decade that the sunspot-weather correlation has made a comeback in a more sophisticated and much diminished form. The rise, fall, and partial rehabilitation of sunspots as a cause of terrestrial weather is a little-known but illuminating story.

I suppose we should begin the story by pointing out that throughout most of recorded history the idea that there were spots on the sun would have been regarded as anathema. Pythagoras taught that the sun was at the center of the universe, a pure embodiment of the elemental fire. Later Greek scientists and astronomers, while they postulated that the sun circled the earth, also believed that it could have no blemish of any kind. One of the great shocks to Western science, then, was the discovery that there are small dark spots that appear and disappear periodically on the surface of the sun.

Western astronomers first became aware of sunspots with the invention of the telescope in the early seventeenth century. The actual historical facts are a bit murky, and there are four individuals (the most prominent being Galileo) who seem to have been the first to see the spots with the new instruments. The coincidence of the development of the telescope and the mention of sunspots in scientific writings has led to the belief that sunspots cannot be seen with the unaided eye* and that the contemporaries of Galileo were the first to find them. The historical record disproves this general impression. Sunspots

---

*Once again, I caution readers never to look directly at the sun. Please see my Author's Note.

were seen by observers in many parts of the world—in fact, as we shall see shortly, almost anyone who cared to observe the sun closely over long periods of time would notice the presence of spots.

The reason that these observations did not get much attention is very simple. Sunspots were not supposed to be there. The teachings of Aristotle, raised to the level of dogma by some scholastic philosophers, made the Greek idea of a perfect sun a main tenet of medieval science. If your ideas about the universe tell you that there is nothing to see, it's unlikely that you'll expend much effort searching. Modern zoologists, for example, do not devote much time to looking for unicorns. Furthermore, even if an excluded object is found by accident, its actual existence may be doubted. So for quite a while scientists did not bother to look closely at the sun, and they ignored the few reports of sunspots that reached them.

Historians, however, have found a large body of observations indicating the existence of spots on the solar surface long before the telescope was invented. The earliest recorded sighting dates back to about 300 B.C., when Theophrastus of Athens (oddly enough, a student of Aristotle's) is supposed to have reported one. Observations with the naked eye were usually made when the sun was low on the horizon and obscured by a dust cloud of some sort. In such circumstances it is possible to see large spots on the solar surface. A typical set of sightings was recorded in Russian chronicles in 1365, when people looking through the smoke of extensive forest fires noticed dark spots on the face of the sun. A similar sighting in France in A.D. 807 was taken to be an omen of the death of Charlemagne; it was referred to as a "defect in the sun."

In those parts of the world where the teachings of Aristotle were unknown or taken less seriously than in medieval Europe, the situation was quite different. Between 28 B.C. and A.D. 1638 Chinese astronomers described and recorded no fewer than 112 sunspot episodes. Less complete records also exist in both Japan and Korea, so there is no doubt that such sightings were taken seriously in the East. Arab astronomers also reported a number of such events throughout the Middle Ages. The record is clear, then—the discovery of sunspots did not wait upon the telescope. Even after its invention, Johannes Kepler, the man who discovered the modern laws of planetary motion, saw a sunspot on May 18, 1607, and attributed it to a transit of the planet Mercury across the face of the sun—anything but admit spots on a perfect countenance!

The telescope did finally succeed in removing such prejudice. Yet after the existence of sunspots had been accepted, very little progress was made in understanding what they were until early in the present century. Several reasons account for this delay. To begin with, motions of the spots were a little boring. A spot would appear, move slowly across the face of the sun for a couple of weeks, and then disappear around the edge—nothing more exciting.

Again, no one had a reliable notion of how the sun was created, so no one had any inkling that sunspots might be important to the understanding of solar processes. For all anybody knew, sunspots might have no more to do with the workings of the sun than bits of debris on a river have to do with the laws of fluid mechanics. In the nineteenth century some fanciful ideas arose, based on the notion that the sun had a cool center (a place where humans could live) that was shielded from the fiery outer coating by a layer of clouds. In this scheme, the spots were taken to be holes in the cloud cover, and the eminent astronomer John Herschel (the son of William Herschel) went so far as to suggest that a clever observer with a telescope could look down the bore of the sunspot and see the countryside underneath! So secure was the judgment of the professional astronomers about the pointlessness of sunspot studies that the most important discovery in solar physics in the nineteenth century was made by a pharmacist.

Heinrich Schwabe was born in Dessau, Germany, in 1789 and spent part of his youth working as an assistant to the family apothecary before going to Berlin to study pharmacy. While at the university, he acquired what became a lifelong interest in astronomy, which he pursued as a hobby after he returned to Dessau to take over the family business. He thought that one contribution an amateur astronomer could make was to record data carefully over long periods of time to see if there were any planets (other than Venus and Mercury) between the earth and the sun. The way to detect such planets, of course, is to look for dark spots making regular transits across the sun's face. Such transits had already been charted for the known planets, and astronomers in the nineteenth century felt that other planets, as yet undetected, could be discovered by this sort of search.

But this plan is not without difficulties. If you are going to be searching for a dark spot that appears regularly on the sun, you have to take account of the fact that there are many dark spots appearing there irregularly—the sunspots. In 1826 Schwabe started to keep very exact records of the appearance of sunspots, with an eye to picking out eventually the spots caused by the regular transit of planets. This procedure a modern scientist would call "separating the signal from the noise."

In 1829, at the age of forty, Schwabe sold his pharmacy and began to devote himself to astronomy full-time. As his data accumulated, he began to notice a certain pattern in the appearance of sunspots. There seemed to be significantly more sunspots in some years than in others, and the recurrences seemed to come in a cycle. For example, if a given year witnessed a maximum number of sunspots, eleven years later another maximum would be recorded. In 1843, with data from two such cycles available, Schwabe announced his discovery.

The response of the scientific community to this unexpected finding was typical. It was totally ignored for almost a decade. Only in 1851, at the urging of Alexander von Humboldt, did serious attention begin to be paid to Schwabe's data. His findings were quickly verified, and he became an honored member of the astronomical community.

Once the cyclical nature of the appearance of sunspots was established, it was possible to go back through the historical record and find confirming evidence. The record for the last two centuries is shown in Figure 3.1. The conclusion is inescapable—the appearance of sunspots during this time frame has, indeed, been cyclical.

Schwabe's discovery forces us to confront two mysteries: what causes sunspots, and why do they appear in this eleven-year cycle? Like the earth, the sun is surrounded by a magnetic

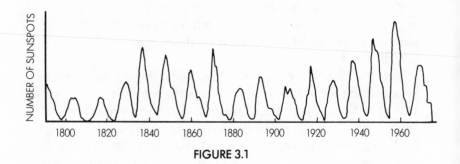

FIGURE 3.1

field. In the sun, this field reverses direction every eleven years. If this state of affairs existed on the earth, the north magnetic pole would spend eleven years in Greenland, then eleven in Antarctica, then back to Greenland, and so on. In addition, it has been found that the magnetic field of the sunspots themselves is typically 10,000 times stronger than that of the general solar magnetic field, a fact that suggests that the origin of sunspots is somehow tied up with magnetism.

The temperatures in the sun are so high that collisions between atoms are violent enough to tear electrons away from their parent nuclei. Consequently, the material of the sun is what physicists call a "plasma"—a mixture of positive and negative electrical charges. A plasma has, overall, electrical neutrality: there are as many positive as negative charges in it, and unlike what is found in ordinary matter, these charges are not tied together in atoms but are free to move around independently.

Plasmas like those found in the sun have an important property: lines of magnetic field are "locked in" to the material, so that if the plasma moves, the magnetic field lines are dragged along with it. There are strong forces in the sun that cause the plasma to move—the upwelling of heated material to the surface, for example, or the rotation of the sun itself. Any movement will distort the magnetic field, and the field lines are dragged along. Horace Babcock of Mt. Wilson Observatory argued in the early 1960s that by far the most important motion of the solar plasma is caused by the differential rotations of the sun. Observations show that the material at the solar equator rotates more quickly than material near the poles. It is as if each time the earth rotated Florida moved a little farther to the east than did Maine. The rigidity of the solid earth prevents this from happening, of course, but on the sun there is no similar restraining force.

Suppose we start with a normal magnetic field such as the one shown on the left in Figure 3.2, below. That the material at the equator moves to the "east" more quickly than material near the poles means that after a while the field lines will be distorted, as shown on the right. As this process goes on, the

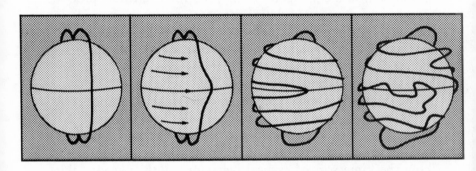

FIGURE 3.2

field lines begin to wrap themselves around the sun. The best analogy to this process would be to think of looping a rubber band around a pencil and then rotating the pencil. The rubber band will wrap itself around the pencil much as the magnetic field lines wrap themselves around the sun. At this point the other motions of the solar plasma become important, for the upwelling of warmer material from under the surface begins to cause irregular distortions in the field lines, as shown on the right. These irregular distortions, which you can think of as being analogous to the popping of the rubber band in our analogy, are what we see as sunspots.

According to a current theory of the nature of sunspots, their dark color is attributable to magnetic effects. The strong magnetic fields at the surface prevent the normal upwelling of hotter material from the sun's interior, making the region around the field cooler than its surroundings. Although both the spot and its surroundings are very hot by our standards (roughly 4,000° and 6,000°, respectively), the spot is cooler and therefore appears dark against its brighter background.

The eleven-year cycle corresponds to the time that it takes for the plasma motions to distort the solar magnetic field. After one cycle, the solar magnetic field again assumes the form shown on the left in Figure 3.2 but with the opposite polarity (i.e., if the first time around the top of the drawing corresponded to the north magnetic poles, the second time around it would correspond to the south). The whole process repeats, and eleven years later we're back where we started. In this picture, there are actually two solar cycles—the eleven-year sunspot cycle and the twenty-two-year cycle, which corresponds to the time between the situations when the direction of both the sunspots and the magnetic field is the same.

The existence of something like the eleven-year sunspot cycle seems to exert a strange influence on the human mind. No sooner does such a phenomenon come to be known than there is an almost irresistible urge to find other things in nature that show the same sort of cyclical behavior. With sunspots, this search began even before the cycle had been established.

Probably no other aspect of solar behavior has generated more controversy than claims to prove the correlation of weather with the sunspot cycle. We have already mentioned William Herschel's study of the influence of sunspots on the price of grain. By 1870, it was claimed that the following quantities (among others) showed correlation with the eleven-year cycle:

1. Air pressure in India (it was supposed to be lower at sunspot maximum)
2. Temperature in Scotland (lower at maximum)
3. Storms in the Indian Ocean (more common at maximum)
4. Rainfall depth of the Great Lakes (highest at maximum)

In this century, as the idea of the influence of sunspots on the weather gathered momentum, many more potential correlations were added to the list. Various phenomena in the upper atmosphere (such as the concentration of ozone) were linked to the sunspot cycle, and worldwide measurements of rainfall, storms, atmospheric pressure, and temperature seemed to agree with the nineteenth-century conclusions. Yet at the time of writing this essay, almost none of this sort of evidence is believed by scientists.

This raises a question frequently heard in discussions of science. How is it that the accepted view of a particular phenomenon can change from one decade to the next? Is "scientific truth" malleable? Does it change like fashions in clothes?

This is a fundamental sort of question. It compels us to think about what constitutes proof. There are two components to any scientific proof: experimental or observational evidence and theoretical understanding. The standards of proof vary depending on what mix of these two components is presented for evaluation.

At one extreme, we have episodes in the history of science like the verification of Einstein's theory of general relativity in 1919. In this case, a beautiful, coherent, fully developed theory of gravitation made certain predictions about the bending of light near the sun. When Arthur Eddington verified this prediction in 1919, the scientific community was willing to accept the theory wholeheartedly. Indeed, even today there are only two solid experimental tests of general relativity, although new experiments are in the advanced planning stage. This example makes it clear that when there is a clear picture of *how* a particular effect works thanks to the existence of a theory, the scientific community does not demand massive experimental documentation for the reality of the effect.

At the other (and far more typical) extreme, the situation is one in which statistical evidence accumulates until a majority of observers will agree that an effect is real, even though there is little or no theoretical understanding of why it should be so. The link between smoking and lung cancer falls into this category, as does the verification of continental drift. In neither case is there a comprehensive quantitative theory that connects cause and effect: yet in both cases the statistical evidence is so overwhelming that few people fail to be convinced unless, as in the case of smoking, there are powerful economic forces at work.

When one has to rely on statistical correlations to establish a relation, then, there can be no hard-and-fast rule as to how much evidence is enough. Each individual uses his own judgment and decides for himself when the regularity has been established. The only principle is that the more evidence, the better.

An example will help to make the point. Suppose we want to prove that a particular coin has two heads instead of one head and one tail. If we flipped it once and it came up heads, everyone but the most gullible would reject the argument that this single test had established the two-headedness of the coin. There is, after all, a 50 percent chance that a normal coin will come up heads on one flip.

Pretty much the same argument would be used if the coin came up heads two, three, or even ten times. The probabilities of a normal coin showing this sort of behavior are $\frac{1}{4}$, $\frac{1}{8}$, and $\frac{1}{1028}$, respectively. None of these are overwhelmingly improbable. But what if it came up heads thirty times? The odds against this are one in a billion. I suspect by this time some observers would be willing to say that the coin was two-headed. By fifty times (odds: one in a quadrillion), we would be strongly tempted to say that the claim had been established, but one could NEVER be 100 percent certain. A normal coin *could* come up heads fifty times in a row. This uncertainty is part of the nature of statistical argument.

With these considerations in mind, we can turn our attention to the kinds of evidence and counterarguments that have been advanced when people try to define the influence of sunspots on the weather. The only way one could reasonably expect to establish a solid statistical correlation between the solar cycle and the weather would be to monitor some meteorologic feature (temperature, rainfall, etc.) and show that it exhibited a regularly recurring pattern every eleven years. Unfortunately, detailed and reliable weather records for most parts of the world are to be had only for the last hundred years or so, the records in only a few places going back a century or two longer. For all practical purposes, then, any attempt to establish worldwide weather patterns on the basis of meteorologic records must be confined to data gathered in the last one hundred years. But one hundred years corresponds to nine eleven-year cycles. In the terms of our analogy, we can flip the coin only nine times. In the early decades of this century when many of the claims for sunspot correlations were made, the arguments were much flimsier, since often the data used spanned only one or two cycles (i.e., the coin was flipped only once or twice).

We can get some idea of what was going on by looking at the rise and fall of one of the claims. A weather station was established on Lake Victoria about 1900. One of the functions of the weather station was to measure the depth of the lake at periodic intervals. When the depth measurements were plotted as a function of time, a result like the one shown in Figure 3.3 was obtained. Suppose you looked at this curve in 1920. It would show a clear cyclical behavior with a period of roughly eleven years. If you were reckless, you might publish a paper claiming that the depth of Lake Victoria showed correlation with the sunspot cycle. The empirical evidence would seem to back you up, and you might even make something of a name for yourself in scientific circles. But you would be wrong.

The reason why this should be so is not hard to understand.

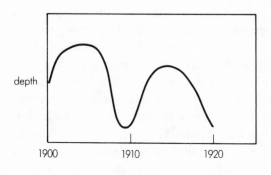

FIGURE 3.3

Anyone who sets out to correlate anything with solar activity will have two criteria in mind. First, the potential effect must be one that fluctuates. There would be no point, for example, in trying to correlate sunspots with something constant like the radius of the earth. Second, the investigator is most likely to pick an effect that will go through a couple of cycles during a human lifetime (i.e., an effect that people are likely to realize is cyclical). This means his attention will be focused on fluctuating phenomena whose scale of variation is between a few years and a few tens of years. For the sake of definiteness, let's say we will examine only those phenomena with a cycle of five to thirty-five years.

Once we have established this basis, we can ask the most important question in statistical analysis: what is the probability that the result we see could be obtained purely by chance? One way to think of this question is to imagine a row of thirty open boxes, each labeled with a number between five and thirty-five. The box labeled "9," for example, corresponds to an effect that changes with a period between nine and ten years. Suppose we throw one marble at the row of boxes. The chance that it will fall into any given box is one in thirty. There is, in other words, about a 3 percent chance that a random throw will put the marble in any given box.

An analogous situation applies when we consider weather data. If we base our analysis on a single fluctuation, then *any* weather index has a 3 percent chance of exhibiting a period in *any* of the yearly intervals, purely by chance. Furthermore, since we are correlating weather with sunspots, we will count our analysis a success if the period turns out to be either eleven or twenty-two years. The random probability that a result will fall into one of these two boxes purely by chance is two out of thirty, or one out of fifteen.

It is obvious, therefore, that a single cycle cannot be used to establish a correlation any more than a single flip of the coin can establish two-headedness. Clearly, one must look at more than one cycle. But that is equivalent to throwing more than one marble into the row of boxes. If we throw two, there is still a probability that, purely by chance, both will wind up in the eleven- or twenty-two-year box. This probability is just twice $\frac{1}{30}$ multiplied by $\frac{1}{30}$, or 1 in 450. This is roughly the probability of flipping a coin and having it come up heads nine times. Our intuition tells us that this is something that will surely happen every once in a while.

But the claimant's situation is even worse than that because of the circumstance known as the *a posteriori* selection of data. The method of calculating probabilities outlined above applies only to the case of predicting the outcome of throwing two marbles into the boxes. In weather analysis, on the other hand, the situation is that of having the data already gathered —the marbles are, so to speak, already in the box. It is tempting to argue in the case of Lake Victoria that since there is only 1 chance in 450 that this particular result could be due to random causes, it must represent a real effect. But the point is that this probability is exactly the same as that of getting any result whatsoever.

An analogy will make this argument clear. Suppose that instead of the two-marble-thirty-box experiment, we had 450 rows of thirty boxes laid out on the floor and that we walked along throwing two marbles into each row. When we finished, we would expect to find one row of boxes in which both marbles sat in the box labeled "11" or the box labeled "22." Therefore, it is not reasonable to pick out this particular row after the experiment has been completed and maintain that it proves the marbles must fall into one of these two boxes.

Many numbers could be used to characterize the weather. We could, for example, use the levels of Lake Michigan or Lake Geneva as our index just as well as the level of Lake Victoria. Each lake would correspond to one row of boxes in our example, and the analysis of each lake's level would correspond to throwing the marbles into that particular row. If we had data on the levels of 450 major bodies of water, we would expect that one of them would show an eleven- or twenty-two-year cycle, purely by chance. It happens that Lake Victoria is the one, but as subsequent events demonstrated, there is nothing universal about the result.

Once this aspect of statistical analysis is understood, you realize that it would be amazing if different weather indices could not be found to correlate with the sunspot cycle, especially when the data extend only over a couple of decades. When you consider that temperatures, frequency of storms, ozone levels, and atmospheric pressure at many points of the earth's surface give us data that we can use for "boxes" in attempting analyses, it is no wonder that some of them will give positive results. What the history of this century shows is that virtually all the claims of this sort were based on data that could have been the result of chance and therefore failed to hold up over a longer time/space.

The only way in which this particular problem can be handled is to collect data over many cycles. If we threw four marbles instead of two in our box-and-marble analogy, the odds that all the marbles would wind up in one of the boxes labeled 11 and 22 by chance fall from 1 in 450 to about 1 in 50,000. With eight marbles, the odds against increase to more than one in a billion—a level at which most people would begin to acquire some confidence in the data. Confidence in a sunspot-weather correlation would require fairly precise data taken over eight or more cycles *at least*.

The lesson in this reasoning is that even in 1920 people should have known better than to claim that the level of Lake Victoria showed a correlation with the sunspot cycle. I know of no better way to drive this point home than to look at Figure 3.4, which shows the data from 1900 to the present. That two cycles don't establish a pattern is painfully evident in the extended data.

The result of all of this is that today only one weather pat-

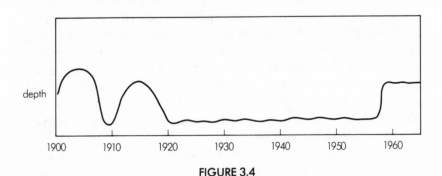

FIGURE 3.4

tern—a twenty-two-year drought cycle in the western United States—is studied seriously for a correlation to sunspots. In this case, the data obtained by studying tree rings extend back into the seventeenth century and hence cover many cycles.

It has been said in jest—and by more than one joker—that *anything* can be correlated with sunspots if one tries hard enough, even the level of women's skirts. Having nothing better to do one rainy spring morning, I decided to see whether this remark had any validity at all. I repaired to the stacks of the University of Virginia main library, to the shelves where back copies of magazines are stored, and I conducted my own "research" in sunspot analysis.

The rules of the game were as follows: I looked up the anniversary issue of *The New Yorker* magazine for a given year. This is the issue that has on its cover a very supercilious young man, clothed like an early-nineteenth-century dandy, looking through his elegant lorgnette at a butterfly. The cover is run every year about the end of February and provides a convenient marker in the back issues. I started leafing through that issue and took the first three ads for women's dresses that showed a full-length photograph or drawing of a model. (The pantsuit craze of the late 1970s played havoc with data gathering.) With a ruler I measured the distance from the model's waist to the hemline of the dress or skirt and the distance from the waist to the foot. Dividing the former by the latter, I obtained a dimensionless number that measures the percentage of the waist-to-foot distance covered by the skirt. The average of the three numbers obtained in this way gave me the data point for the year.

The data from 1926 to 1980 are shown in Figure 3.5. The successive dips in the graph (representing periods when the fashion was for short skirts) correspond roughly to the flapper era, the postwar period, and the miniskirt boom. The result is clear: a twenty-two-year cycle is seen superimposed on a general trend for skirts to get shorter.

As was true of the level of Lake Victoria, my data show a clear correlation with the sunspot cycle through two cycles. Naturally, all the arguments I urged before will apply to the hemline effect: there are hundreds of indices that could be used

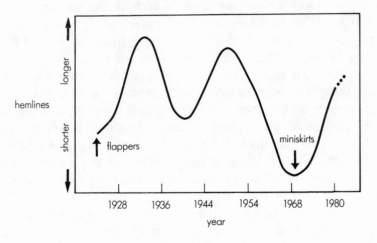

FIGURE 3.5

to describe fashions, so it is statistically inevitable that one of them will match for a couple of cycles. I suspect, however, that most readers wouldn't need this sort of argument to see the inherent ridiculousness of claiming that this correlation is a genuine regularity over time. It's a good thing to keep hemlines in mind the next time you hear statistical arguments that seem incongruous or ridiculous.

FOUR

When the Sunspots Disappeared

L OUIS OF BOURBON, King of France, fourteenth of that name, was born in 1638, ascended the throne five years later, and died in 1715. During this long reign he set new standards for opulence for the courts of Europe, building the palace at Versailles and making French culture and the French language dominant throughout the world. So brightly did his reputation shine that he earned the nickname of "Roi Soleil," the Sun King. Molière, Racine, and La Fontaine were just a few who enjoyed his patronage. And although his death shortly after the War of the Spanish Succession left France near bankruptcy and his policies did not change the conditions that led to the French Revolution, he nevertheless left a rich legacy of artistic and intellectual achievements for later ages to enjoy.

Lately, it has become clear that the Sun King enjoys yet another distinction. By one of those strange coincidences that are too farfetched to appear in anything but real life, during the reign of Louis XIV, the appearance of spots on the face of the sun came to an almost complete halt.

The story of how this sudden stopping and restarting of the solar cycle came to be discovered is unusual, for it depends largely on the interpretation of historical records. This is not something that physical scientists feel comfortable doing. For one thing, we are not trained to deal with documents and have very little idea of the pitfalls that await the unwary in this field of research. What is more, the opinion of modern scientists is that since we are now capable of making better observations, conducting better experiments, and doing more complete calculations than ever before, we have no reason to go back and look at what our predecessors did several hundred years ago. It is only occasionally, as when the question arises whether the sunspot cycle has been steady in the past, that we are forced to study their work closely. This reluctance to consider historical evidence played a major role in the story I am about to relate —a story that is quite unlike those surrounding other scientific discoveries.

The scientific community, as we saw earlier, may have been slow to digest the work of Schwabe and the facts of the eleven-year solar cycle, but once it did, the idea of a regularly recurring process in the sun became deeply entrenched in the accepted view of things. It is not difficult to imagine that a ponderous and complex body like the sun might exhibit regular short-term behavior any more than it is hard to grasp that a huge body of water like the ocean can produce regular small-scale features like waves. By the end of the nineteenth century, then, when the attention of astronomers was turning to the question of the sun's composition, the solar cycle came to be regarded as a valuable clue to the nature of that star.

In 1893, a man named Walter Maunder was superintendent of the solar division of the Greenwich Observatory in England. By virtue of his position, he was in his day an influential solar astronomer—certainly not a fringe figure in this field. In going through old books and astronomical journals, he came to the conclusion that the solar cycle had not been in evidence between 1645 and 1715—a period of some seventy years. He published these results the following year in a paper entitled "A Prolonged Sunspot Minimum." The paper was greeted by total silence and lack of interest, much as Schwabe's paper had been a half century earlier. For thirty years Maunder tried to get people to take his findings seriously, but without success.

One can think of several reasons why Maunder's suggestion of an anomaly in the solar cycle was ignored. For one thing, his argument relied heavily on the historical records of seventeenth- and eighteenth-century astronomers. While there is no particular reason to doubt that very capable astronomers were practicing their craft at that time, skeptics argued that the lack of records on sunspots then does not necessarily indicate that the spots weren't there. The prevailing notion at the time was that sunspots were clouds in the solar atmosphere; as such, they might simply have been ignored. To use a phrase that has come into vogue in the debate over extraterrestrial intelligence, absence of evidence does not necessarily constitute evidence of absence.

There was, moreover, a deeper reason for the scant attention paid to Maunder by his colleagues. The early twentieth century was the time when the picture of the sun as an enormous fusion-powered energy generator was beginning to develop. It is suggestive to think of the sun as an enormous locomotive speeding down the tracks. To someone looking at a locomotive from the outside, the most important feature is the steady turning of the wheels; likewise, to someone looking at the sun, the steady cycle of the sunspots might seem its outstanding feature. Yet in both images the energy used in producing the outward appearance is a small fraction of the total generated.

Suppose that after years of hard work you had developed the beginnings of an idea of what was actually going on in the locomotive and that you had some notion of how the furnace actually worked. Suppose further that just as all this was becoming clear, someone came along and told you that there was evidence (perhaps questionable) that the wheels stopped turning every once in a while—that the steady cycle now visible did not extend indefinitely into the past. Your first reaction would undoubtedly be the same as that of Maunder's contemporaries. You would ignore the unwanted complication and get on with the main business of the day, which was understanding the workings of the furnace itself.

The upshot was the general assumption that the sunspot cycle had always been a part of the sun. This conventional wisdom certainly prevailed in astronomy until the middle of the 1970s, when Jack Eddy, now at the National Center for Atmospheric Research in Boulder, Colorado, began to give the whole subject a serious review. Thanks to his persistence and open-mindedness, we now have a clearer and truer picture of the past behavior of the sun.

As you will remember, sunspots were one of the first items of interest seen in heavenly bodies after the introduction of the telescope. The spots were reported in books and journals still extant; there can be no question about the sightings. What Maunder noticed was that during the seventy years between 1645 and 1715 almost no sunspots were reported in the scientific literature, even though this was a period of intense study of all astronomical objects. He suggested that the reason no one had discovered the solar cycle before Schwabe was that during much of the time when such a discovery could have been made there were no sunspots to be seen.

To me, the most impressive fact about the scientific journals of the seventeenth century is not the absence of sunspot reports but the kind of thing that was said when one was described. For example, in 1671, Giovanni Cassini, of the Observatory of Paris, commented on his own report of sighting a sunspot: "It is now twenty years since astronomers have seen any spots on the sun, though before that time, since the invention of the telescopes, they have from time to time reported them."

So significant was this observation felt to be that the editor of the *Philosophical Transactions* of the (English) Royal Society wrote a report in which he described the appearance of the last sunspot seen some eleven years previously and went on to say: "At Paris the excellent Signior Cassini hath lately detected again Spots in the Sun, of which none have been seen these many years that we know of."

The point of these sample quotations is simple. Cassini was one of the best observational astronomers of his time—he discovered the gaps in the rings of Saturn now known as the Cassini divisions. The *Transactions* was the journal of the Royal Society, the most prestigious scientific group in Europe. It is most unlikely that scientists of this caliber would bother to report sunspots if these appeared in the hundreds (as they do now), and it is doubly hard to suppose that a journal of that stature would comment on fresh sightings if, as some maintained, the sunspots were there all the time but were not considered worthy of notice.

Frankly, the two passages quoted above should have been enough to establish the existence of a prolonged dearth of sunspots. They convince me. But as we shall now see, they constitute only one piece of evidence among many for what is now called the Maunder Minimum in solar activity. It turns out that the Minimum can be seen in many astronomical records and even in tree rings!

When charged particles from the sun enter the earth's magnetic field and are deflected toward the poles, they interact with molecules in the upper atmosphere to produce the flickering lights characteristic of the aurorae. The connection of aurorae to the sunspot cycle is well established, though indirect.

At the peak of the solar cycle, when there are many sunspots present, there are also many more particles streaming out from the sun. These particles, called the solar wind, flow around the earth's magnetic field on their way out of the solar system. A particularly violent burst of particles (such as that associated with a large solar flare) will produce the aurora by a process similar to that by which a beam of electrons produces a picture on your TV tube. We expect, therefore, that the aurora will be common during periods of high solar activity, less common when the sunspots are absent.

Today, the Aurora Borealis appears almost nightly in extreme arctic regions, and anywhere from twenty to two hundred times a year in regions of northern Scandinavia and North America. The farther south one goes, the more infrequent the aurorae become, with an expected average of five to ten per year at the latitudes of London and Paris. They do appear farther south than this occasionally—indeed, I saw one once in the Blue Ridge Mountains of Virginia.

Aurorae are mentioned in historical records. In Figure 4.1 we show a sketch of the frequency of such reports from observers in northern latitudes from 1500 to the present. The Maunder Minimum is clearly evident in this set of data and is indicated by the arrows in the figure.

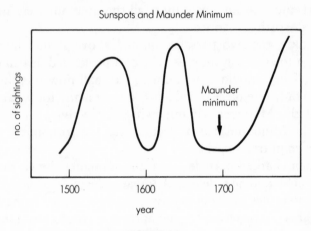

Sunspots and Maunder Minimum

FIGURE 4.1

The interpretation of this result is not as straightforward as it might appear at first glance. That aurorae were reported more frequently after 1715 may be strongly influenced by social factors. As we have mentioned, aurorae are seen most commonly in northern latitudes that are less densely populated than their southern neighbors. In addition, the scientific revolution, with its emphasis on the observation of nature, came slightly later to the northern parts of Europe than to the south. Thus, you would expect the number of reported aurorae to increase with time simply because more people were looking at the sky and recording what they saw.

Having said this, one must add that Figure 4.1 does not afford much support to those who argue that the aurora sighting can be explained completely by social conditions. If the aurorae were always to be seen in roughly their present numbers and if the only change in the reports resulted from increased interest in celestial observations, we would expect a smooth monotonic increase in the sightings from the Middle Ages to the modern period. One possible curve of this type is shown as a dotted line in the figure. It seems clear that the rapid increase in sightings after 1715 must be due, at least in part, to an actual increase in aurorae and therefore an increase in solar activity after that date.

Yet another line of historical evidence has to do with the appearance of the sun during a full eclipse. When the moon blocks out the disc of the sun, a halo of light known as the corona is seen. By far the most important aspect of the corona at times of normal solar activity, such as the twentieth century, is the presence of enormous streamers radiating away from the solar surface. These are caused by the magnetic disturbances associated with sunspots. It follows that if an eclipse should occur during a period of little or no solar activity, none of these spectacular streamers would be visible. This opens up a third possibility for investigating the Maunder Minimum historically, for there were no fewer than sixty-three solar eclipses between 1645 and 1715.

Unfortunately, as so often happens with historical evidence, things aren't that simple. The main concern of astronomers during those seventy years was to understand the motion of bodies in the solar system. To them, solar eclipses provided a marvelous way of testing their ability to predict the orbital motion of the moon, and hence their observational powers were primarily expended on determining the exact time of each eclipse. For this purpose a total eclipse was not necessary—indeed, for various technical reasons a partial eclipse was preferable. Thus there was hardly any motive for astronomers to travel away from their observatories to view a total eclipse. Today, of course, when astronomical attention centers on the structure of the sun itself, it is worthwhile to travel enormous distances and set up temporary laboratories to make measurements during totality. In the seventeenth century, a total eclipse was likely to be seen by professional astronomers only if it happened to come within sight of an established observatory. As it happened, only eight of the sixty-three total eclipses on the schedule were actually so observed, and three of these occurred after 1700, when the solar cycle was about to recommence.

Even so, if we look at this limited sample, we find remarkable agreement among observers. The corona is described as a narrow ring of light around the moon's disk, whose color was a "dull and mournful red." It is reasonable to conclude that these observers saw none of the fireworks associated with sunspots. And although this conclusion can be attacked like the other historical data, we feel that Jack Eddy put it best when he wrote: "I suspect that anyone who has ever seen the breathtaking beauty of the corona with the unaided eye will find these excuses [i.e., historical error or neglect] entirely inadequate."

The historical evidence that is hardest to interpret is the records of nontelescopic sunspot sightings in the Orient. We have already discussed some of the reasons why such records are not available in Europe, but there are other reasons why sightings with the naked eye must be studied with caution. For one thing, only very large spots or groups of spots can be observed in this way, and there is no guarantee that such phenomena will occur during periods of high solar activity. After all, a few sunspots appeared even during the Maunder Minimum. Furthermore, sunspots can be observed only if a thick haze permeates the air, so that some areas (such as northern China, with its frequent dust storms) are more likely to produce sightings than others. Finally, even in the Orient the process of recording was subject to strong social influences. For example, during periods of war or great social turmoil the office of the Astronomer Royal might cease to function for decades at a time. Frequent sunspot sightings were taken to be bad omens —the harbingers of the downfall of a dynasty—and hence might or might not be recorded, depending on the political situation. To some extent such vagaries can be dealt with by comparing records from different countries (e.g., China and Korea) that might not be undergoing political upheaval at the same time.

A further uncertainty, typical of what is encountered in dealing with old writings for any purpose, is that it is not always possible to produce an unambiguous interpretation of what the writers set down on paper. For example, in A.D. 352 the following observation was made: "According to observations made by Chang Ch'ung at Liang-Chou, the sun was a dazzling red, like fire. Within it was a three legged crow. Its shape was seen sharp and clear. After five days it ceased." This probably refers to a sunspot, but it takes a certain amount of educated guesswork to make the identification.

With all of these hazards in mind, David Clark of the Royal Greenwich Observatory compiled available records from China, Japan, and Korea. He found several gaps in the records and made certain of three that can probably not be explained by interference from social causes. They are, therefore, presumably due to changes in solar activity similar to the Maunder Minimum. These three occurred around the seventh, thirteenth, and seventeenth centuries, respectively.

If we take this result seriously, we arrive at the notion that the Maunder Minimum may not have been an isolated event and that the sunspot cycle may be an irregular and sporadic feature of solar behavior.

Suppose you had to make a decision about the reality of the Maunder Minimum based on the evidence reproduced so far. To decide intelligently, you would first have to grapple with the historical record. Much of it is pretty weak, particularly the reports of sunspot sighting in the Orient and of aurora sightings in Northern Europe. On the other hand, the writings of seventeenth-century scientists would seem to you, as to me, strong evidence. As I said, I would accept the Maunder Minimum solely on the basis of the testimony given by Cassini and the editor of the *Transactions*, for I can see no way of interpreting their remarks except by acknowledging the existence of a long, sunspot-free period in their time.

Fortunately, we do not have to rely entirely on the historical record. Thanks to another example of the interconnectedness of science, direct evidence for the Maunder Minimum was found in, of all places, the tree rings on Douglas firs in the Pacific Northwest.

To understand this odd linkage, we must recall that during periods of high solar activity the solar wind is relatively intense. When it blows by the earth, it tends to distort the earth's magnetic field in much the same way that an ordinary wind distorts a tree. This distorted magnetic field, in turn, tends to deflect charged particles away from the earth. These particles, called cosmic rays, rain down on the earth's atmosphere from space, and the ones we are interested in come primarily from stars other than the sun. Thus we have a situation in which low solar activity results in a higher intensity in the stream of these kinds of cosmic rays striking the earth.

Now, when a cosmic ray enters the upper atmosphere, it can collide with a nucleus to produce a spray of debris including a neutron or two (see Fig. 4.2). This neutron can then go on to strike the nucleus of another atom, nitrogen, knocking out one

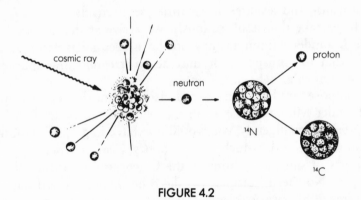

FIGURE 4.2

of its protons. The result of this chain of events is that a nitrogen atom in the atmosphere is converted into an atom whose nucleus contains six protons and eight neutrons—an atom that has the chemical properties of the element carbon but with a difference. This atom, called carbon-14, has a nuclear mass of fourteen units as opposed to normal carbon, which has twelve (six protons and six neutrons). Atoms of carbon-14 mix with ordinary carbon in the earth's biosphere and are incorporated into living matter.

Like atoms of ordinary carbon-12, those of carbon-14 are taken up by living plants and incorporated into molecules, including those that make up the rings of trees. Once incorporated, the carbon-14 begins to undergo radioactive decay. It has a half-life of 5,600 years, which means that after that time half of the nuclei of the original carbon-14 atoms will have decayed, after 2,800 years three-fourths will have decayed, and so on. Thus, if we count backward along the tree rings until we find one that was formed 2,800 years ago and measure the amount of carbon-14 in the ring, we can be sure that this is precisely one-fourth of the amount of carbon-14 that was in the wood when it formed. The ordinary carbon-12, on the other hand, does not decay, so what is in the wood now is what was there at the beginning. Analyzing the amount of these two isotopes of carbon that are in the tree ring now, then, gives us a way of deducing how much carbon-14 there was in the environment when that wood was formed. And this, as we have seen, tells us something about sunspots.

The best way of applying this principle is to examine old trees. There are, after all, many trees still standing which were in existence during the Maunder Minimum. All through the Minimum, these trees were adding growth rings each year and incorporating carbon from the atmosphere into their fibers. Measuring the carbon-14 content in these trees, conveniently segregated into annual increments by the growth rings, we infer the cosmic-ray flux in past centuries. This, in turn, tells us what we want to know about the sunspot activity.

In Figure 4.3, we show data on carbon-14 amounts in Pacific Northwest Douglas fir trees over the past eight hundred years; the modern telescopic data on the solar cycle are superim-

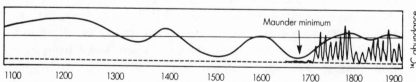

FIGURE 4.3

posed. The data shown are "upside down," the higher carbon concentrations being in the downward direction, because an increase in carbon-14 corresponds to a decrease in solar activity. This method of presentation has the advantage of having increased solar activity always represented by the upward direction on the graph.

The carbon-14 verdict is clear! The Maunder Minimum shows up as a clear excursion in the tree-ring measurements. A second minimum of the same type, known as the Sporer Minimum, is seen around 1500; and a third, somewhat less pronounced, occurs in the fourteenth century. This last one is called the Medieval Minor Minimum. Both the Sporer and Medieval Minima correspond to gaps in the Oriental naked-eye sunspot records discussed above and hence give credibility to that particular piece of historical data. This direct measurement of the carbon-14 uptake in tree rings gave the *coup de grace* to those who doubted the other historical evidence, which supports the existence of the Maunder Minimum.

But once we accept the idea that the sunspot cycle is far from regular, that it has stopped and started erratically in the past, we are confronted with a very difficult puzzle. How can a body as massive as the sun, one that has poured out a steady stream of energy for over four billion years, exhibit such unsteady and unpredictable behavior? This question remains one of the major problems faced by solar scientists today.

At a deeper level, though, the story of the Maunder Minimum illustrates a very important philosophical point about the way science works. The assumption that the world has always been more or less as we see it today is a natural one to make. Ever since the great battles between some of the early geologists, who argued that the processes operating in the earth today have operated for all time, and their colleagues, the catastrophists, who argued that unusual events like Noah's flood had dominated history, scientists have shied away from any hint that special, unrepeatable events have occurred in the past. The attitude that favors stability is seen most strongly among earth scientists, but to some extent it pervades all the natural sciences. Confronted with hints and partial evidence of anything like the Maunder Minimum, the gut reaction is to say,

"There must be something wrong here," especially if the evidence presented comes from unfamiliar sources such as historical documents. It took overwhelming evidence of this sort, as gathered by Jack Eddy, to bring about a change of heart.

The saga makes you wonder how many more surprises are lurking in those dusty scientific journals.

FIVE

Clouds

C LOUDS ARE SO MUCH a part of the atmospheric land-
scape that we tend not to notice them unless we are
afraid it will rain. Yet they form an ever-changing
spectacle overhead, and there are few occupations more peaceful than lying on the grass under a shady tree, watching them
change as they float by. As it happens, there are a number of
lessons in science you can learn by doing just that. Was there
ever a better excuse for whiling away a lazy summer afternoon?

Like most people, I learned the names of the clouds in grade
school, and since the names were Latin (cirrus, cumulus, etc.), I
assumed they dated from antiquity. It came as a great surprise,
when I started reading up on clouds, to find that our present
naming system dates only from the early nineteenth century.
Apparently no one before that time had thought to christen the

regularities in cloud structures. Even someone of the stature of Aristotle, who made a meticulous catalog of coastal life and wrote a book on the weather, never thought of classifying clouds, though he classified almost everything else. I suspect that the ever-changing shape of the clouds accounts for this oversight—after all, why try to classify something that changes all the time?

It wasn't until 1803 that a rather unusual Englishman, Luke Howard, wrote a paper entitled "On the Modifications of Clouds" in which a modern naming scheme was set forth. No one knows why anybody suddenly became interested in clouds after centuries of neglect. Howard came from an ordinary Quaker background and went to a school where, in his words, "I learnt too much of Latin grammar and too little of anything else." He was by profession a druggist, and historians speculate that he became interested in watching the sky during 1783, when the eruption in Japan of a large volcano called Asamayama caused spectacular displays all over the world.

The classification scheme proposed by Howard contains the skeleton of modern systems; it divides clouds into two types— clouds that are layers and clouds that are heaps. The former bear the name *stratus*, from the Latin for "stretched out." The latter are called *cumulus*, from the Latin for "heap" or "pile." You can easily verify that clouds do fall into these two groups by glancing at the sky from time to time during the next few days.

Howard's classification scheme was taken up and refined by those studying the new science of meteorology, but a new impetus for the detailed study of clouds came with the development of manned flight and particularly from the needs of military pilots in World War I. As we shall see, clouds serve as markers of local weather conditions and are consequently very important to pilots.

We may note in passing the surprising amount of our knowledge of the natural world that has sprung from the needs of the military. Most of our knowledge of the way beaches are formed, for example, comes from work started during World War II, when the U.S. Navy suddenly found itself required to conduct amphibious operations and put large numbers of troops ashore on islands in the Pacific. The distinction between "pure" studies of nature and military research is not nearly so sharp as some social commentators and some scientists like to think.

In any case, the modern scheme for classifying clouds is illustrated in Figure 5.1 below. Each of the four main types is shown, and some of the subdivisions also. The different groups correspond to the different composition and mode of formation of each form of cloud.

As you can see at a glance if you have spent any time cloud watching, the forms in the sketch only hint at the rich diversity visible in the sky; a detailed description of the possible shapes is only to be found in publications like the two-volume *International Cloud Atlas*. For our purposes, though, there will be quite enough on our plate if we try to understand the basic cloud types and ignore the details of the subdivisions recognized by professionals.

The physical process behind the formation of clouds—the condensation of water out of the air—is familiar enough. Anyone who has watched a jet of steam coming out of a tea-

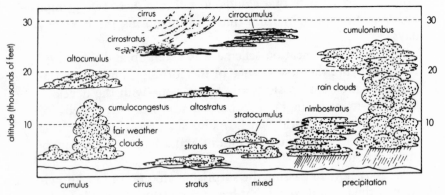

Schematic of General Cloud Forms at Varying Altitudes

FIGURE 5.1

kettle or the dew falling on the grass has seen the process at work. How this condensation takes place will occupy us at length later on, for it is an example of one of the most interesting phenomena in nature. But for our first look at clouds, we need only know that it is possible for water that is held in the air in the form of molecules to come together in the form of tiny droplets.

Start by thinking about the molecules in an open pan of water. At any temperature above absolute zero, the molecules will be undergoing an intricate dance, colliding constantly with each other. In these collisions, some molecules will gain energy and move faster; others will lose energy and move more slowly. Thus, while the average velocity of the molecules in the pan of water is determined by the temperature, there will always be some moving faster than the average. You can think of this as analogous to the market economy: there is an average income for any group, but some members of the group will be rich and others poor.

When a molecule approaches the surface of the water, it feels an attractive force exerted by the other molecules around it—a force that tends to pull the molecule back into the body of the fluid. This attractive force must exist because a drop of water tends to hold its shape, and without some sort of internal molecular attraction it couldn't do so. The next time it rains after you wax your car, notice how the water beads up on the clean surface as the fluid pulls itself together: that is a direct verification of the existence of an internal attractive force between water molecules.

If an average water molecule approaches the surface, then, the force of the other molecules is enough to keep it from leaving. But if one of the *faster* molecules approaches the surface, the molecule may escape. After a while, the air above the pan will contain many escaped molecules, which will themselves be undergoing collision with other molecules in the air. In the language of physics, we say there is a certain vapor pressure characterizing the water in the air; it is defined as the pressure that would be exerted by the water molecules if all the air were removed.

Vapor pressure is actually a universal property of materials

—it is not restricted to liquids like water. A very few molecules will escape even from a block of steel, and there will be a vapor pressure characteristic of those molecules. Astronauts have even measured a tiny vapor pressure at the surface of the moon—it corresponds to the escape of atoms from rocks on the surface.

A pan of water exposed to the air will therefore lose some molecules, but will also gain some as molecules already in the air return to the fluid. The same is true of a drop of water suspended in the air—molecules leave and molecules return. If more return than leave, the drop grows. If the reverse holds, the drop shrinks. Thus, the fate of a water droplet depends on how many water molecules there are in the air around it.

The amount of water the air can hold depends on the temperature. The hotter the air, the faster the molecules move; the more violently they collide, the more "elbow room" there is between the air molecules and the more water molecules can squeeze in. At any temperature, there is only so much room, only so many water molecules the air can hold. In the jargon of meteorology, the number of water molecules actually in the air, divided by the number that could theoretically be accommodated, is called the relative humidity. When the relative humidity is high, the air is holding almost as much water as it can. Consequently, a droplet will take in almost as many molecules at its surface as it loses and will therefore take a long time to evaporate. If the droplet happens to be sweat on your skin, its failure to evaporate and carry off energy will make you uncomfortable, and you will say that the weather is muggy.

When the relative humidity is low, as it is in the desert, a droplet will lose a large number of molecules for every one it gains and will therefore evaporate quickly. You can even get a dry rain—a situation in which the air is so dry that the raindrops evaporate in the time it takes them to fall from a rain cloud; so none actually manage to reach the ground. I remember being told by one old-timer of a rain in eastern Montana that wet his hat but not his boots. I suspect there was a little leg-pulling going on there, but there is certainly a molecule of truth in that tall tale.

Clouds have their origin in the water molecules in the air. The story starts when air comes in contact with the sun-warmed earth. This patch of air will become warmer and less dense than the air above it and will consequently start to rise.* As it rises (usually in the form of a bubble), it finds itself in an environment of lower pressure, so it expands. The expansion, in turn, causes the bubble to cool regardless of the temperature of the surrounding air. The farther the bubble ascends, the cooler it gets. As it goes up, the bubble of course carries its original complement of water molecules; but as it cools down, the relative humidity increases, because although it has the same amount of water as when it left the ground, the air is capable of holding less the higher it goes.

Eventually, the rising bubble reaches the point where the air can no longer hold the water it has been carrying. What happens next is quite complex, but the result is the formation of a cloud—a collection of water droplets or ice crystals, depending on the altitude and temperature. The vast majority of clouds are formed by water droplets, and we will take it for granted as the norm as we proceed with this discussion.

When water condenses into droplets, it gives up heat. You can see that this must be so by noting that as a droplet grows, it is constantly absorbing fast-moving molecules from its surroundings. The bombardment of these molecules heats the droplet, and the heat is then radiated away into the surroundings. Hence, as the cloud forms, the air around it is heated. This has the effect of increasing its buoyancy and driving it farther up into the sky. As it rises, the air once again expands and cools, forming still more droplets and increasing the size of the cloud.

The formation of a cloud is not an irreversible act. Just as an individual droplet can grow or shrink, depending on the relative humidity of its environment, so, too, can a cloud grow or vanish once it has been formed. For example, if part of a cloud encounters a downdraft, it will be carried downward to regions of higher pressure. In that case, the air in the cloud

---

*For a more detailed discussion of the structure of the rising air bubble, see my book *Meditations at 10,000 Feet* (Scribners, 1986).

will heat up, molecules will leave the surface of the droplets and not be replaced, and the cloud will disappear. The clear spaces that you can sometimes see in a cloudy sky are made this way. They may be spots in which cold air is descending, wiping out the cloud as it goes.

Alternatively, the cloud may form where the rising air bubble comes into equilibrium with its surroundings. In this case each droplet gains as many molecules as it loses from its environment, and the cloud is stable. This sort of cloud will be moved by the wind for long distances with little change.

This simple picture of cloud formation explains what is probably the first thing you notice about clouds when you start watching them: no matter how complex the cloud structure, its bottom is always approximately flat. From the billowing summer cumulus to the dark, threatening nimbus, this rule holds. The reason is clear: the temperature of the rising air depends on how much it has expanded, and this, in turn, depends on the pressure of the surrounding air. Thus, every rising bubble in a given area will start to condense into drops at the same altitude, which explains the flatness of the cloud layer. (There are, of course, exceptions to this rule in unusual situations.)

It really doesn't take much water to make a cloud. A small summer cumulus but a few hundred yards to a side may contain no more than 25–30 gallons of water—about enough to fill a bathtub.* When a cloud touches the ground, it is called fog. If you walk 100 yards through a typical fog, you will come into contact with only about half a cubic inch of water—not enough to give you a decent drink. Clouds really are insubstantial things!

The clouds in the sky can serve as clues to the motion of the air. The fluffy, separated cumulus clouds characteristic of a warm summer afternoon represent small, scattered rising air currents. Stronger currents, carrying large masses of air, can "punch through" the point where the condensation starts and push the cloud upward to great altitudes, particularly if they are aided by the release of latent heat. Meteorologists who study the tropics have found that these towering cumulus

---

*Typical water contents in clouds run in the range of 0.1–3.0 grams per cubic meter, or 10^{-7}–3×10^{-6} gallons of water per cubic foot of cloud.

clouds play a major role in taking heat from the earth's equatorial region and carrying it, by wind circulation high aloft, to the poles.

Stratus clouds, on the other hand, come about when air masses are lifted upward over a large region. this may be a result of large-scale updrafts from the ground; it may also happen when one air mass is gently lifted up over another high in the atmosphere. This process gives rise to one of the more familiar types of stratus cloud—the high, feathery cirrus that pressages a change in the weather. These clouds start to form under the circumstances shown in Figure 5.2. Warm, moist air starts to move into an area from the left and is driven up over the mass of cold air in front of it. As the warm air is lifted up, it expands, and clouds form by the process already described. The first hint that this is happening—the harbinger of the storm—is the cirrus formation at great altitudes, at the very tip of the system. Cirrus means "fiber" in Latin, and the name is an apt description. Formed at altitudes above 30,000 feet (six miles), these clouds are composed primarily of ice crystals. Because of this, you sometimes see strange effects as the sun shines through them—halos, sun dogs (bright spots in the sky about 22° away from the sun) and other optical effects. All

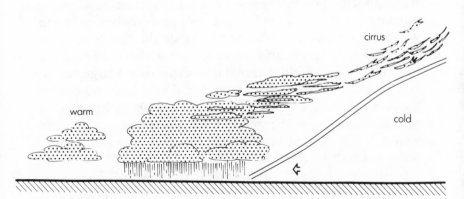

FIGURE 5.2

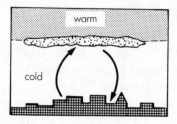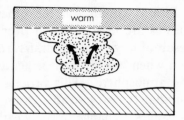

FIGURE 5.3

these arise from the interaction of the sunlight with the ice.*

As the warm air in the weather front continues to advance, more of it is pushed up, and layers of stratus clouds are formed. Eventually, enough droplets of water form in the cloud to cause rain: the weather change presaged by the cirrus clouds has arrived. If it is cold enough, the water in the cloud will crystallize, and we will get snow, but from the point of view of the cloud this is only a small difference.

The mixed-cloud categories—heaps and layers together— usually result from the presence of stable layers in the atmosphere. As pictured in Figure 5.3, above, this is a layer of warm air sitting on top of a layer of cold air, the cold air being in contact with the ground. Since cold air is more dense than warm air, no forces are acting to change the situation; it remains static. Termed an inversion, such a stable warm layer can cause serious health hazards if it occurs over a large metropolitan area. Pollutants are trapped in the cold air and cannot leave, and the result is smog. Until something happens to change the inversion, the smog will keep getting worse as more materials are injected into the air. In some cases, it actually becomes life threatening.

Inversion layers effectively block the upward motion of heated air. When air heated by contact with the ground

*An excellent source of information on the complex displays arising from ice is to be found in Robert Greenler's *Rainbows, Haloes, and Glories* (Cambridge University Press, 1980) or in my book *The Unexpected Vista* (Scribners, 1983).

reaches the inversion layer, it will usually cool and descend, forming what is known as a convection cell. If it cools enough at the top for condensation to take place, a layered strato-cumulus cloud will form. It will be flat, like a stratus cloud, but will have a relatively small area, like a cumulus.

If the inversion occurs at higher altitudes, other types of mixed clouds are formed. Sometimes you might see a tall cloud that has been formed by a powerful updraft but that has been stopped by the updraft running into an inversion layer. Such a cloud will have a flat top or perhaps be shaped like an anvil, as shown to the right of Figure 5.3. In either case, the cloud gives a very good visualization of the inversion layer.

With this basic understanding of cloud formation, we can get down to the serious business of enjoying cloud watching. Since it is cumulus clouds that characterize good weather, they are the ones most likely to be the subject of leisurely examination. The first thing you'll notice about a cumulus cloud if you watch it for a while is that it doesn't hold its shape. It changes continually, its towers of billowing white disappearing and others growing before your eyes. This occurs because in most cases more than one rising air bubble contributes to each cloud. As each bubble reaches the condensation level, it forms a column within the cloud. If there is a wind, the column is eventually blown away, and the relatively tenuous upper parts disappear first. While this is happening, the cloud may be on the move, so that when the next bubble arrives, it forms a column at a different spot within the cloud. If part of the cloud happens to drift into a region where the air is moving downward, it will be broken up as the moisture is reabsorbed and the droplets evaporate. It is this endless shuffling about of water vapor in the atmosphere that makes cloud watching so entrancing. The next time you are in a plane above the cloud layer, look around and see if you can spot the billowing towers that mark the place where air is coming up and the clear gaps where it is sinking.

Another interesting cloud phenomenon that is particularly striking from an airplane is the result of the interaction be-tween the air and a mountain chain. It is best seen in places like the Appalachians, where there are many ridges inter-

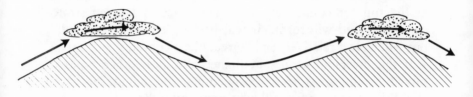

FIGURE 5.4

spersed with valleys. On a fine day, you will often see a row of puffy cumulus clouds along the top of each mountain ridge and clear skies over the valleys, as sketched in Figure 5.4, above.

What is happening here is that the presence of the mountain forces air upward, as shown. As it enters the regions of lower pressure, the air cools and condensation occurs. This forms the cloud at the top. As the air crests the ridge and starts down again, it is compressed and heated, and the water droplets that condensed on the uphill slope evaporate and go back into the air. The cloud disappears. The result is a "lenticular" (lens-shaped) cloud perched at the top of the ridge. An important point to remember about this situation is that the wind is blowing *through* the cloud and the individual water droplets in the cloud are being continually interchanged. The cloud may be likened to a lake through which a river flows—it always has the same amount of water in it, but the water is never the same water. In just the same way, the cloud always contains the same number of droplets, but the droplets are always different ones. This means that the lenticular cloud will remain stationary at the top of the mountain no matter how hard the wind is blowing. In this regard, it differs from ordinary clouds, which tend to be highly mobile.

A fascinating variation on this theme is occasionally seen on the downwind side of a mountain or a hill. As sketched in Figure 5.5, air blowing over a hill is forced into a wavelike motion on the downwind side. Without going into details as to why this occurs, I may say that the upshot is similar to the flapping of a flag in a stiff breeze. The effect of the wave structure is that a given volume of air will move into, then out of, regions of higher altitude. It can happen that at the top of each wave the conditions exist for the formation of a lenticular cloud. The result will be, as shown, a series of such clouds stretching parallel to the hill. I remember seeing three such clouds on the eastern side of the Bighorn range of the Rocky Mountains near Sheridan, Wyoming (a town that, incidentally, has the best and most spectacular rest stop on the entire Interstate system). The clouds remained stationary for well over a half hour—the time it took me to eat lunch and let the kids use the playground. I stayed for an extra half hour because I had never seen anything like that sky spectacle before—the clouds never moved. Amazing what you can see if you keep your eyes peeled!

A similar effect will occur on the leeward side of almost any mountain range if a low cloud layer is being blown against the mountain on one side but it is clear on the other (Fig. 5.6). In those conditions, the clouds come spilling over the low points of the mountains, for all the world like water flowing over a dam. When the clouds start down, they disappear as the air heats and reabsorbs the water vapor. The result is a slow spill of cloud ending with wispy tendrils. There is enough motion in the tendrils to keep the scene from being static, and the operation continues long enough to make watching most enjoyable. The spilling fog also marks out the motion of the colder air moving down into the valley, so that the way the air moves is clearly visible. When I was a graduate student at Stanford, I considered that the inconvenience of having a stu-

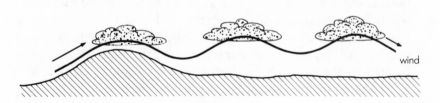

wind

FIGURE 5.5

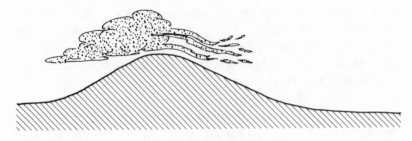

FIGURE 5.6

dent office on the top floor of the building was more than outweighed by the marvelous views of the Pacific clouds coming over the Santa Cruz Mountains and into the San Francisco Bay area.

Speaking of San Francisco, it is the home of what is probably the most famous cloud in America—the fog that comes in almost daily from the ocean through the Golden Gate, at times covering the great bridge entirely, sometimes covering everything but the towers, but always providing a photographer's dream at sunset. Known technically as an advective fog, this cloud is formed when air moves for a long time over a cold surface such as the waters of the Pacific. Eventually, the air will be cooled to the point where droplets start to form, even though it remains at sea level. The fog extends from the sea, where it is coldest, up to the height where the normal air temperatures are high enough to prevent condensation. Advection, in other words, is the reverse of the normal cloud process, where height and cold are synonymous. Nevertheless, that the fog rolling in through the Golden Gate and the wispy collection of ice crystals that herald an approaching storm are formed by the same physical processes is as good an example as I know of the universality of the laws of nature.

SIX

When Clouds Go Bad

UGUST 2, 1985: It had been a hot day in Dallas—temperatures at the airport had reached 101° F. during the afternoon. Now, as evening approached, it was cooling off. By six o'clock, the evening rush was in full swing. The skies over the airport were filled with planes. Inside each came the familiar litany "The captain has put on the seat-belt sign in preparation for our final approach...." The passengers were putting away their books and papers and getting ready to land. Some were going home, others starting a visit, yet others making connections with other flights—a typical scene at a major airport.

The weather appeared to be unexceptional, if not optimal. Cumulus and cirrus clouds were scattered over the area, and some heavy thunderstorms loomed near the Texas-Oklahoma border. Just before six o'clock a small thunderstorm developed near the airport. Locally, the rain was heavy, but it wasn't anything to worry about.

Within the thunderstorm cloud, however, something was happening that was to prove fatal to some of the passengers about to land. For reasons we do not fully understand but that may have involved the evaporative cooling discussed in chapter 5, a mass of cold, dense air was forming. This relatively heavy air began to sink rapidly to the ground. Its downward progress can be traced by noting what happened to the series of aircraft that came in to land on runway 17L.

At 6:01, American Airlines 351 crossed the outer markers for the runway at an altitude of about two thousand feet. Almost at once it encountered heavy rain and loss of airspeed, slowing from 200 to 175 mph in about 20 seconds. The pilot compensated for these conditions and brought the plane to a safe touchdown at 6:04.

The next plane in line to land was a small Lear jet of the type used by private corporations. It crossed the outer markers at 6:03 and, like its predecessor, encountered heavy rain and sudden loss of speed. Because of this loss the plane dropped below the correct flight path, and the pilot had to apply power to get back to the position needed to bring the craft in safely. The Lear jet touched down at 6:05. As we shall see, the Lear jet was the first plane to encounter the massive blob of cold, falling air directly.

Next in line was Delta 191, stopping over on its way from Fort Lauderdale to Los Angeles. There is a bit of folklore among pilots that if the plane in front of you has managed to get down safely, yours will, too. Unfortunately, no one in the plane or the control tower knew that when Delta 191 crossed the outer markers at 6:04, the cold air had hit the ground and was swirling outward from the point of impact. The first intimation of disaster came when the aircraft ran into strong downward winds at 6:05:33. Because of the aircraft's position, its right wing was pushed down more than the left, causing the plane to roll. The pilot compensated for this sudden movement, and Delta 191 continued on its way.

The next obstacle came from two bursts of very high tailwinds rushing at speeds close to 60 mph. Again, as we shall see later, this sudden blow made the aircraft slow down and lose altitude. Since it was already near the ground, there was no room for maneuver, and at 6:05:52 the wheels touched down in a plowed field across the highway from the airport. After bouncing twice on the field as the pilot fought to regain control and get the plane back into the air, Delta 191 reached highway 114, at which point it was tilting slightly to the left. One engine struck a passing car, five light poles were knocked down, and the plane started its last fatal skid across the field in front of the runway. It wound up colliding with a large water tank, spilling debris across the runway on which it had been scheduled to land. The toll for the accident: 133 dead and 31 injured.

While these events were taking place, the flights next in line were being told to "go around"—to cut off the landing procedure and get back up in the air. American 539 was the plane just behind Delta 191. It crossed the outer markers at 6:06 at 2,000 feet and almost immediately began climbing. At 3,000 feet it met the last portion of descending cold air, experiencing some strong buffeting and rain but no serious loss of speed or altitude.

This narrative is particularly sobering—even frightening—in an age when so many of us fly so often and so confidently to distant points. Aircraft accidents are rare, of course, and statistics show that one is safer going by plane than taking the same journey by car. But when accidents do happen, they usually kill large numbers, and I for one admit that, statistics or no, I find it hard not to think of such things as the Delta 191 crash whenever my plane comes in to land.

Scientists and engineers concerned with air safety are naturally not content with mere apprehension. Their aim is to analyze each accident, find out what caused it, and think of what might be done to prevent its recurrence in the future. After the Dallas crash, their thoughts turned to the behavior of clouds and the winds that can burst out of them. But if we are to understand how these people think, we must also understand how it is that an airplane manages to stay in the air in the first place.

It has long been known to physicists that when air is moving quickly, its pressure is lower than when it moves more slowly. One familiar example of this effect may be seen in a fireplace on a windy night. When the wind gusts—that is, when the wind speed at the top of the chimney is high—the flames and the sparks seem to be sucked upward. This is a result of the air in the room being pushed up through the chimney toward the lower pressure outside.

When air flows over an airplane wing (see Fig. 6.1), a similar situation develops: the air that moves over the curved top of the wing has to travel farther than that which goes along the bottom and thus moves faster. The pressure on the top of the wing is therefore lower than that on the bottom, so that there is a net force pushing upward on the wing. Called *lift*, this force is what counteracts the downward pull of gravity and keeps the plane in the air.

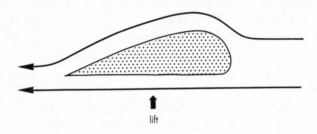

lift

FIGURE 6.1

An important aspect of the generation of lift is that it depends on the relative speed of the airplane and the wind. For example, the lift on a wing moving through still air at 50 mph is exactly the same as the lift on an aircraft sitting on the ground in a 50-mph wind. That is why you sometimes see news photos of light planes that have been tossed around by a severe windstorm, even though they were sitting innocently on the ground. By the same token, if a plane is moving east at 200 mph with respect to the ground but has a headwind of 20 mph, the lift developed on its wings is the same as it would be if it were traveling at 220 mph through still air.

Here, in a nutshell, is the reason why variable winds close to the ground are so dangerous to airplanes. If the plane keeps moving at the same power setting, a sudden gust of wind can drastically increase or decrease the lift on the wings. This, in turn, can lead to sudden changes in altitude of the type experienced by the planes coming in to Dallas on that fateful evening. But how do such strong and variable winds arise?

A decade ago most meteorologists would have denied the existence of the descending bubble of cold air that led to the Delta 191 crash. That we now know something—and are learning more—about such phenomena is largely due to the efforts of one man—Theodore Fujita, who was born and trained in Japan but who has, since 1956, been associated with the University of Chicago.

Fujita is an internationally known expert on tornadoes; he is the author of the Fujita scale, a scale used by meteorologists to judge the strength of a tornado and the damage it has caused. The Fujita scale plays a role for tornadoes similar to that of the more familiar Richter scale for earthquakes—it enables us to give a numerical estimate of the intensity of the disturbance.

My own introduction to Fujita's work came in the early 1970s, when I was a visiting scientist at Argonne National Laboratories near Chicago. He came there to conduct a seminar on his work, and given the importance and severity of tornadoes in the Midwest, he attracted a large and appreciative audience. What struck me most about Fujita's lecture wasn't his discussion of the mechanics of tornadoes, although that was very interesting, but that the world's leading expert on tornadoes, who had spent a great deal of time chasing them around the globe, had never actually seen one in action. It seemed a little sad to think that someone so deeply concerned with the admittedly rare phenomenon should be denied a sight of it. (I'm happy to relate that in the years since the seminar the anomalous situation has been rectified.)

In the course of studying the effects of winds, Fujita often surveyed the scene of a storm from the air. In 1974, he noticed a rather unusual pattern of tree damage near the town of Beckley, West Virginia. What he saw can be imagined by looking at Figure 6.2. On the left is shown the sort of pattern you might expect to see from the swirling winds of a tornado. The tree

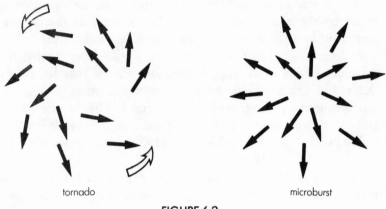

tornado   microburst

FIGURE 6.2

trunks ought to lie in a roughly circular pattern corresponding to the path of the wind. On the right is shown what was actually seen. The tree trunks lay in what Fujita came to call a "starburst" pattern, all pointing away from a central core. The best way to explain this effect is to imagine that a blast of air came down vertically and then rushed outward from the point of contact; it is the sort of pattern you see in a sink when you turn on the faucet hard.

At the time, this notion was not given much credence among meteorologists. The general opinion was that although it was entirely possible that downdrafts could develop in clouds, they would be so diminished by their passage through still air that by the time they reached the ground they would have lost most of their energy. They certainly would not have enough left to push down a tree or affect the flight of an airplane.

But as time went on, Fujita found more and more of his patterns, especially in midwestern cornfields, where the felled stalks showed the path of the winds very clearly. I remember seeing one slide, taken in 1977, that showed a barn with a slanted tin roof standing next to a large cornfield. A straight path of broken canes stretched for hundreds of yards away from the barn, and the pattern was such that it could only be explained by a downward burst of air being deflected by the sloping roof into the field.

The existence of these downward currents is no longer doubted. During a long series of studies in Colorado in the late 1970s, many examples of their action were seen, a couple close to the main research station. In fact, says Fujita, "Once I was almost blown into a lake, so I have proved their existence."

Fujita called his air currents downbursts and split them into two categories: macrobursts, in which the outward winds extend 2.5 miles or more; and microbursts, in which they extend for less than 2.5 miles. In relation to aircraft safety, it is the latter that are important, for their relatively small size makes them very difficult to detect.

The kinds of air movement that affect an airplane are divided into two general categories—turbulence and wind shear. Turbulence produces the familiar bouncing and jostling motion of the airplane, but though it makes passengers uncomfortable, it seldom causes the plane to stray much from its path. Wind shear is defined as any wind motion that alters the lift force and thus causes the plane to gain or lose altitude. The microburst is a special example of wind shear. Another example is a sudden gust of wind that causes a change in the relative speed of the air over the wing.

You can begin to get some idea of how a microburst affects low-altitude flight by considering the simple wind pattern sketched in Figure 6.3. The wind is shown coming down vertically from a cloud, then moving out horizontally. A plane entering this wind pattern from the left will suddenly encounter a strong headwind and find that its speed relative to the air has increased. From the reasoning detailed above, it follows that lift will go up, as well, so that the plane will start to climb. To compensate, the pilot will reduce power, slowing down the plane. Then, when the plane reaches the central region where the downward flow is strong, lift will decrease, and the plane will be pushed down. On the right-hand side of the trajectory, the plane suddenly finds itself with a strong tailwind. Its speed relative to the air, and hence the lift, will drop just as the pilot needs all the lift possible to come back up. If he is unlucky, he may not be able to compensate, and the microburst will have claimed another victim.

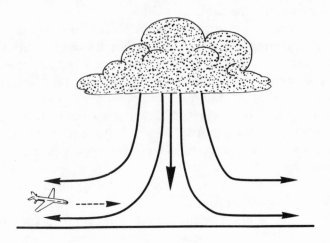

FIGURE 6.3

In very large microbursts such as the one at the Dallas airport, the situation is more complex. Instead of a smooth outward flow from the point of contact, the burst may well develop the type of vortex structure shown in Figure 6.4. These vortices have been photographed in the western United States, where the dust carried by the wind makes the swirls visible. They have also been reproduced in the laboratory by Fujita, using smoke to etch the wind patterns.

An aircraft entering the vortex structure will be subjected to very rapid changes in wind speed. Also, since the distance across the vortex is roughly the same size as an airliner's wingspan, a situation may occur in which one wingtip is being pushed up while the other is being pushed down. It is believed that the sudden roll of Delta 191 was caused by just such an effect.

The vortex structure of complex microbursts has another effect. As an airplane passes through the vortex, it encounters sudden shifts in wind direction. For example, at the point labeled A it will meet a strong headwind; at B, an equally strong tailwind. Thus, the craft will undergo violent changes of lift within a very short time.

FIGURE 6.4

With these facts about microbursts and their influence on flight, we can turn to Fujita's reconstruction of the events of 1985 at the Dallas airport. Figure 6.5 shows the burst at four stages of development, and superimposed on each stage is the flight path of one of the four planes discussed above.

As American 351 made its approach, the downward burst was well above the flight path; the craft encountered strong winds and heavy rain but no wind shear. A few minutes later, the Lear jet came in on the same path. By that time the downward-moving burst had almost reached the ground. The jet entered the region of strong downward wind and suffered sudden loss of altitude, as shown. The pilot was able to compensate for this loss, fly through the rest of the burst, and land safely.

A few minutes more and the burst had hit the ground and was spreading outward in the characteristic vortex pattern. These were the conditions that awaited Delta 191. It passed through several vortices and suffered a sudden roll and equally sudden changes of lift. The pilot was able to compensate for all this. But when the plane got into the region of outflow, at the point labeled *A*, the loss of lift occasioned by the tailwind

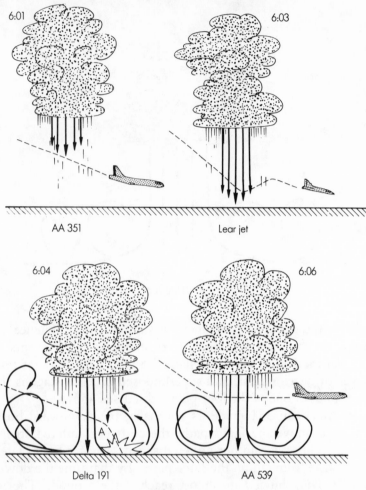

FIGURE 6.5

was too much to handle, and the fatal loss of altitude followed.

A few minutes later, the microburst had fully developed. Because of the crash, American 539 was waved off and managed to climb to an altitude of 3,000 feet before entering the burst. It thereby rose above the heart of the vortex structure and avoided the worst of the changes in wind direction. Aside from being bounced around, it suffered no damage at all.

This detailed description of the effects of one microburst at a major airport was put together by Fujita when he was called in to investigate the accident. It is a very clever piece of detective work, based on the Weather Service radar, the aircraft flight recorders, the control tower records, and conversations with members of the flight crews involved. What it shows pretty conclusively is that microbursts constitute a major hazard to airliners. It also shows that the one effective way of dealing with a microburst is to avoid it. Like major thunderstorms and other hazardous weather conditions, the microburst, if detected, can be dealt with.

"If detected" is the crucial phrase here, for the early detection of a microburst is extremely difficult. Unlike its huge cousin the macroburst, the microburst need not originate in a major storm or a large cloud. A small, isolated thundershower was quite enough to cause destruction at Dallas. This means that one can't deal with microbursts by shutting down airports. If major airports like O'Hare or LaGuardia were closed every time there was a thunderstorm in the vicinity, it would wreak havoc with the airline traffic throughout the nation. As it is, travelers on the East Coast know that planes are often not allowed to take off until their place in the landing line at La-Guardia has been set. The only practical way to deal with the problem is either to discover a way of predicting when a burst will occur or to find the means of detecting the burst itself.

Either choice poses a technical problem. Bursts are hard to detect directly because the radar systems in use around the country for monitoring the local weather are not designed to pick up something as small or as localized as a microburst. The reason is simple: normal radar works by measuring the difference in reflections from materials of different density. The water droplets in clouds, for example, send back a signal different from that of dry air, so clouds show up clearly on the radar screen. You have no doubt seen such radar pictures on television weather reports. Similarly, large drops in falling rain produce an image different from that of small drops in clouds, so rain can be located by radar.

But the density of the air in a microburst does not differ greatly from that of the surrounding air, even though in the microburst the air is colder. The difference in signal on the radar detector is very small; for all intents and purposes, the microburst cannot be separated from its surroundings.

Add to this the fact that air-traffic controllers have at best but a few minutes to note the downward-moving air before it invades the place where it can do damage and you face a first-class technical problem.

One solution being discussed and tested today is to use the so-called Doppler radar, which measures the speed of the object from which the beams are reflected. Think of it as a sophisticated version of the type of radar used by police to catch speeders. The shift in frequency of the reflected beam tells the police how fast your car is traveling. In the case of the weather radar, the shift in frequency tells how fast the cloud or air mass is moving.

One way of imagining the use of Doppler radar at an airport is sketched in Figure 6.6. A network of radar antennae would

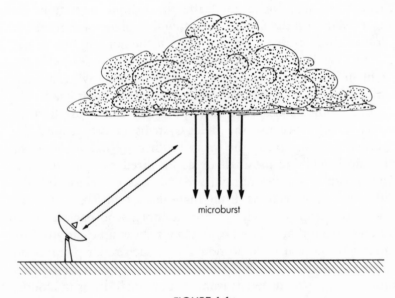

microburst

FIGURE 6.6

scan the sky constantly. If a possible microburst situation developed, the radar system could monitor the vicinity of the danger zone, watching for a fast-moving downward burst of air. If such a burst of air should start as shown, it would register as a sudden small change in frequency of the reflected beam. To work effectively, several radar stations would have to be linked together in order to determine the direction of the air mass. Once the signal was identified, automatic warning systems would enable the controllers to warn aircraft away from the area until the burst had spent itself.

There are a number of obstacles to the deployment of such a system at major airports. For one thing, Doppler radar is expensive—not the sort of equipment to be installed without a thorough test program. More important is the simple fact we still don't know enough about the downdraft and microburst phenomena to be sure that what we install will be the best preventive of accidents. More scientific work has to be done before we really can say what will truly serve our purpose.

To date, two large-scale studies of microbursts have been completed. They bear the acronyms NIMROD (Northern Illinois Meteorological Research on Downbursts) and JAWS (Joint Airport Weather Study). The first, carried out in 1978, used three Doppler radar stations near Chicago. The second, begun in 1982, used three Doppler radars and twenty-seven small meteorologic stations in the Denver area. In the summer of 1986, work started on a similar network in the Southeast. The aim of all these operations was to identify and study downbursts in areas near major airports.

During these surveys many microbursts were seen, and a great deal of valuable data on their properties was gathered. One thing I found surprising was the frequency of the bursts. In the summer of 1982, for example, the JAWS network recorded no fewer than 186. For a phenomenon that was supposed to be rare, this is an astonishing number. It appears that many events that are considered to be ordinary high winds actually come from microbursts.

The results of these studies were in many ways discouraging. They show that the downburst phenomenon is much more complex and multifaceted than was expected. Although the Dallas microburst was accompanied by heavy rain, it turns out that many bursts involve no rain at all. Roughly 80 percent of the microbursts seen near Denver and 30 percent of those near Chicago were of the "dry" variety. Some bursts, moreover, come straight down, whereas others are blown sideways by the wind, which results in an asymmetrical vortex near the ground. Some bursts never manage to reach the ground, but peter out in midair. Sometimes the bursts start to twist on the way down, causing a burstlike outflow on the ground and a tornadolike cyclone aloft. Occasionally, one of the vortices can break loose from the rest and head out across country, for all the world like a tumbling rolling pin made of high winds. Obviously, there is no simple pattern for microbursts; they form a whole class of phenomena that has to be studied in detail in order to be dealt with.

We are equally puzzled when we shift our attention from description to causes. No single type of cloud gives rise to microbursts. They can be produced in towering thunderstorm clouds, of course, but they can also come from isolated rain clouds, with or without a thunderstorm, and from various types of large cumulus clouds, as well. The most picturesque of these Fujita calls the "giant anteater" cloud. It is shown in Figure 6.7. Given this complexity of origin, it's no wonder that

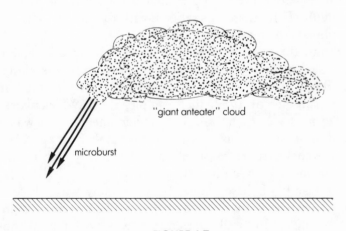

FIGURE 6.7

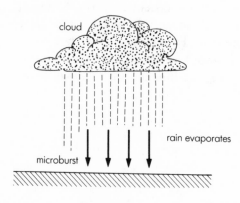

cloud

rain evaporates

microburst

FIGURE 6.8

our ability to predict when a given cloud will produce a down-burst is so poor.

In fact, only one thing about the genesis of the microburst can be stated with assurance. Somewhere a large quantity of air has to be cooled quickly enough so that it starts a rapid descent toward the ground. The most obvious (but not the only) factor to account for this is evaporative cooling. When water evaporates, it removes heat from its surroundings to supply the extra energy needed to pass from liquid to a gaseous state. You splash water on your face on a hot day to cool yourself off. The same effect can occur in clouds.

For example, look at Figure 6.8, above, in which a dry microburst seen in Colorado is sketched. Rain started falling from a cloud but evaporated while passing through the air. The evaporation sucked heat from the air, which then became more dense than its surroundings and sank toward the ground. Had this happened over an airport instead of over rangeland, it could have produced an accident such as that which struck Delta Flight 191.

Such is the status of our knowledge about microbursts. We have seen them, cataloged them, and learned something of the complex systems of causes that produce them. We still lack sufficient knowledge to predict when a given cloud will produce a microburst. Nor do we know enough to put together an effective warning system to protect our aircraft. Until we acquire that knowledge, we will have to be content with the kind of comment Fujita makes when he is asked what one should think about when landing or taking off: "You're safe from microbursts so long as you're above a thousand feet."

SEVEN

What Ever Happened to Hurricane Zelda?

I WAS VISITING the Savannah River Laboratories when I first heard about it. These labs, founded in World War II and run by the Dupont Corporation for the federal government, are the place where much of the serious nuclear chemistry in this country (including the production of both weapons material and isotopes for use in medicine) gets done. Situated on the Georgia–South Carolina border, it is a high-tech wonderland nestling in a blanket of scrub-pine forests.

What caught my attention that day was only peripherally related to nuclear physics. The lab has a complex weather-monitoring system built into it. Every five minutes data on wind direction and speed, precipitation, and so on, are fed from a dozen sites around the installation into a computer, where they are combined with regular reports from the National Weather Service on conditions in the surrounding countryside. The result: an up-to-the-minute picture of what the weather in and around the laboratory is like.

The woman operating the station when I came through seemed to enjoy her work and was anxious to show off her toy. "Give me an accident," she said. It turned out that what she wanted was for me to make up an event involving an accidental release of nuclear materials.

"How about a loss of containment and a release of plutonium?" I answered, thinking of the worst case I could.

She punched a few keys on her console. "How much plutonium?" she asked.

"A few pounds," I said, again imagining the worst.

A few more keys were tapped. "Anything else?" she asked.

So far I had been able to bluff my way through, but my lack of expertise in nuclear chemistry caught up with me. I was forced to admit that I had no idea what else might come out when plutonium was released from a reactor. My host for the visit, a nuclear engineer, came to my rescue with what a typical release might be. The operator punched in a few more commands to the computer, and at once a map of the laboratory and the surrounding area appeared on the screen. A plume appeared near one of the reactors and started to grow. Suddenly the reason for the elaborate weather-monitoring system became clear. Knowing which way the wind was blowing enabled the staff to predict what would happen if an accident were to occur.

As the plume on the screen approached the boundaries of the laboratory (a large wooded area almost 20 miles across), the screen started to blink. A warning signal appeared, telling the operator that the cloud would cross the boundary, when it would do so, what the radiation levels would be when it did, and which state and federal agencies must be notified immediately. I think it even gave the telephone numbers.

I was impressed. In less time than it has taken you to read this account, the system had produced a detailed prediction to guide the recovery from my hypothetical accident. The weather-station staff seemed pleased with my reaction and in the glow of success seemed inclined to be expansive.

"Do you want to see the hurricane?" they asked.

"What hurricane?"

In response, a few more buttons were pushed, and a map of the southeastern United States and part of the Caribbean Sea flashed on the screen. Out to sea, well off the coast of Florida, a tiny little symbol flashed in red. The symbol, shown in Figure 7.1, represents hurricanes—real ones, not hypothetical ones.

FIGURE 7.1

I asked what I have been told most visitors ask when they are shown the symbol: "Will it mess up my flight back this afternoon?" As it happened, it was a few days before this particular storm made its presence felt in the continental United States. But I shall never forget how I came to have advance knowledge of the coming of hurricane Gloria in the fall of 1985.

Gloria was an uncommon happening, because it was the first major storm to hit the East Coast for which highly accurate advance notice was available, and it claimed a high level of public attention as it moved up the East Coast. The coast was fortunate in that Gloria vented most of her fury at sea and caused relatively little damage when she finally hit the land in New York and Connecticut. Nevertheless, Gloria, like earlier storms, changed people's lives during her brief visit. I know of one prominent publisher who canceled a trip to Virginia to avoid the storm. And on the night when there was a chance it would come ashore on the Virginia coast, the motels in Charlottesville, 200 miles inland, were jammed.

During the week that followed, the analysis of the storm and its impact was covered extensively in the news media. I had never thought much about hurricanes, but repeated phone calls from reporters (including one who wanted to know if there was a connection between the spiral shape of the storm and the spiral shape of a galaxy) made me realize that I had been overlooking a very interesting topic. As I found out, the life cycle of a hurricane brings into an integrated whole many striking features of our planet, from its daily rotation to the state of its oceans. And the mechanics of the storm—the way it behaves once it gets going—illustrate some very interesting principles of physics.

The hurricane is one form of the great revolving storms that occur in the tropics. They are characterized by a corkscrewlike flow of air and clouds into a region of low pressure. Europeans learned about their existence from the voyages of Columbus. They appear in all of the earth's oceans except the South Atlantic. In the Orient they are called typhoons; in the Atlantic, hurricanes; and everywhere else, tropical cyclones. They are sharply distinguished from monsoons, which are seasonal flows of wind in Africa and Asia that bring heavy rainfall.

For many people the most intriguing thing about hurricanes is that they are given names. Naming makes it easy to identify and talk about them, of course, but I had some difficulty finding out how the custom started. One story I heard, which I pass along for what it is worth, is that the custom grew out of a best-seller of 1941 by the novelist and lexicographer George Stewart. Entitled *Storm*, it had as characters members of the Weather Bureau who gave storms names—some used the names of girls, others the names of famous generals, and so on. However the practice started, assigning girls' names was not in use until the Second World War, when armed forces meteorologists adopted the practice. In 1953, the random naming was replaced by an alphabetical system by which the first storm of the season bore a name starting with an A, the second with B, and so on. In 1979, the present system, in which boys' and girls' names alternate, was adopted. Gloria was thus the seventh storm of the 1985 season.

If you follow the weather news at all, you have probably noticed that most of the names belong to the first half of the alphabet only. When did you ever hear of a hurricane named Zeke or Zelda? This observation suggests an important truth about hurricanes—they occur in relatively small numbers. Out of more than a hundred weather situations that might develop into Atlantic hurricanes each year, only between five and fifteen do so. This means that it's extremely unlikely we shall ever get past Ophelia. But aside from this reassurance about nomenclature, we want to know the answer to two great scientific questions: what exactly causes a hurricane, and why don't they occur more often? It turns out that we really don't know the answer to this double question. The ability to predict which tropical storm will grow into a hurricane is, at present, outside the reach of science.

Figure 7.2 gives a sketch of the Atlantic Ocean on which some typical tracks of hurricanes are shown. The storms start as mild low-pressure regions (depressions) off the west coast of Africa. Moved westward by the trade winds in the tropics, they cross the Atlantic in a northward curving path. To become hurricanes, they must gain strength during this crossing by picking up energy from the warm surface waters of the ocean. Somewhere in the neighborhood of the Caribbean, the storm turns northward and makes a landfall in the Gulf of Mexico or the eastern coast of North America or else blows itself out over the sea. These possible upshots are shown in the figure.

Confronted with a storm system hundreds of miles across, a system whose normal movements cover a good fraction of the earth's surface, one can raise many questions. Where, for ex-

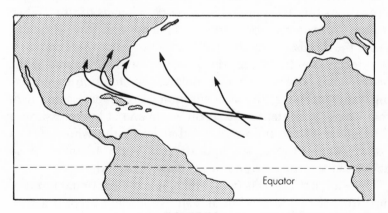

FIGURE 7.2

ample, does the energy to drive such a system come from? After all, the energy in the storm exceeds that of even the largest nuclear weapon: it has to come from somewhere. Why does the wind flow into the central low-pressure area along curved paths instead of in straight lines? Why do the storm tracks curve up away from the equator instead of following the trade winds straight across the ocean? And, to ask the sort of question I love to get my teeth into, why can't a hurricane ever cross the equator?

Let's start with the question of energy sources. As is true of all weather systems on earth, you could say that the ultimate sources of energy for hurricanes are the rotation of the earth and the heat from the sun. These two together create the winds and temperature difference that drive the changes in climatic conditions. The special feature of the hurricane, other than its violence, is that once it starts, it seems to grow and hold together for very long periods of time. It is this energy— the energy that keeps the storm together once it starts—that we want to track down.

The structure of a mature hurricane is shown in Figure 7.3. The hurricane differs from other storms in that it has a warm core—indeed, one of the striking features of the beast is that nearby temperatures do not fall precipitously when it passes by. At lower altitudes, the surrounding air rushes in toward the center of the storm along the characteristic curved paths shown. As this air approaches the core, it begins to rise. When it does so, water vapor starts to condense and form droplets. From the discussion in chapter 5, we know that this condensation forms clouds; indeed, this process is a major source of the heavy cloud cover over the storm area. In addition to supplying water droplets, the condensation also generates the heat that keeps the center of the storm warm and at low pressure; it thus increases the inflow of air that keeps the whole system going. At the top of the updraft area, some 10 miles or so above the sea, the air flows out and away from the core.

Once a hurricane gets going, then, it is the continual input of heat from the condensation of water vapor that keeps it active. The strong winds close to the surface whip up the ocean, creating sheets of spray that serve to increase the area of contact

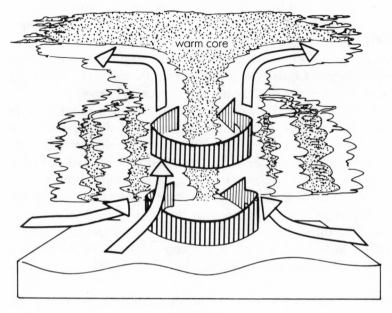

warm core

FIGURE 7.3

between air and water, and this in turn facilitates both the transfer of water and the transfer of heat from the ocean to the atmosphere. You can think of the hurricane as a sort of giant vacuum cleaner moving over the warm surface of the tropical seas, sucking up energy from the water. Not only does it feed on the water by using the heat of condensation to keep itself going, but in the process it actually affects the ocean surface in such a way as to make the process still easier. The conclusion that the ocean is the ultimate source of the storm's energy is borne out by the fact that hurricanes quickly diminish in strength when they start to move over land.

You can get an idea of the amount of energy involved in the simple process of condensation by holding a cold knife blade in the steam that comes out of a kettle on your stove. While you watch the beads of water collect as the vapor condenses on the steel, touch the blade and notice how quickly it heats up. Multiply that blade by the thousands of square miles of air and water that make up a hurricane and you can see how enough energy is derived from this source to power the storm.

As an aside, we should note that condensation is an example of the physical process called a phase change. So important are these processes in modern physics that we will devote the entire next chapter to discussing them. For the moment, we simply note that they provide the hurricane with its energy.

Having solved this particular riddle, we turn to what is, to me, an even more interesting question—why do the winds and the storm move as they do? Why, for example, do the winds entering the storm area follow a curved path instead of falling straight into the low-pressure zone, as you might expect intuitively? And what forces keep up the whirling motion of the storm center? It so happens that the answers lead us to one of the most intriguing areas of physics—the subject of what are called "fictitious" forces. It was considerations of the sort we are about to take up that eventually led to the theory of relativity early in this century.

The characteristic of our planet that causes the curving paths we see in satellite photographs of the hurricane (or any other large storm) is that the planet rotates daily around its axis. To see the point, refer to Figure 7.4. In response to a low pressure

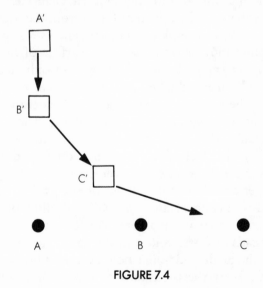

FIGURE 7.4

at the point A, a block of air at point A' is set in motion. It begins moving toward the point of lower pressure, just as air moves into your lungs when you expand your diaphragm and create a low-pressure area inside your chest. While the block of air is on its way, the point A is being carried eastward by the rotation of the earth, so that when the block has reached the point labeled B', the low-pressure zone has moved to B. At that point the block has to undergo a "mid-course correction." The forces of atmospheric pressure now impel it toward the point B, and it dutifully assumes its new direction.

It is easy to see that this process will repeat itself indefinitely: by the time our block of air has reached C', the low-pressure zone will have moved to C; when the block reaches D', the zone will be at D, and so on. The result is precisely what we see in the photographs. As the block chases the ever-moving low-pressure zone, it traces out a spiral path.

In reality, these "mid-course corrections" are taking place all the time, and the path traced out is smooth rather than segmented like the line in the figure. Nonetheless, the idea represented by the figure is correct, and it tells us that the air entering the storm will move in a counterclockwise pattern of circulation. You can test your understanding of what happens by convincing yourself that a similar block of air in the Southern Hemisphere will also trace out a spiral, but one in the opposite (clockwise) direction.

In working out this problem, we have taken the point of view of someone above the earth, someone who could look down on the planet from a vantage point where both the rotation and its effect on motion could be seen. But what about someone who lacks the advantage of such an observation platform? After all, the entire human race, until quite recently, lacked such a vantage point. How, then, does someone on the surface of the earth describe the same set of events we've just discussed?

If you are on the earth, you are not aware of rotation. As far as you are concerned, you are standing on a perfectly stationary, unmoving platform. From your point of view, the air moving into the low-pressure area is simply following a curved path. But if you were a sophisticated observer considering this phenomenon toward the end of the seventeenth century, you would know that Isaac Newton had written down a set of three laws of motion—laws that were supposed to explain the motion of all material objects. The first of these laws, and the only one we need in order to understand what follows, is this: an object at rest will remain at rest, and an object in motion will move in a straight line, unless a force acts upon it.

Go back to our winds: the motion is clearly not in a straight line. The only conclusion an earthbound observer could draw is that some force was acting to cause the wind's spiral movement. The details of this force were worked out by the French mathematician Gustave de Coriolis and is named in his honor. Our sophisticated observer on the earth now says that the inward-moving air deviates from straight-line motion because of the action of the Coriolis force. This force acts perpendicular to the direction of motion of the object being watched and hence causes it to deviate from the type of motion it would have if no such force were present.

There are many other manifestations of the Coriolis force. You may have visited a science museum that had a huge pendulum swinging from a ceiling and had your attention called to the fact that the pendulum didn't always swing in the same plane. The Smithsonian Institution in Washington contains a set of little red blocks arranged in a circle under the pendulum, and every ten minutes or so the pendulum has moved to the point where it knocks over another red block. The crowd invariably cheers when this happens—don't ask me why. The earth dweller's conclusion is that the Coriolis force is acting to push the pendulum sideways as it swings. To an observer in space, the apparent sideways motion arises because the earth is rotating under the pendulum. Either way, the result is the same—the pendulum rotates, and knocks over the blocks.

Clearly, the Coriolis force also explains the shape of the hurricane tracks. When a storm starts moving westward from Africa, the Coriolis force deflects it away from the equator and toward the pole. This contributes to the poleward drift of the storm that we mentioned earlier. When this drift carries the hurricane out of the region of the trade winds (which blow to the east), it is subject to the action of the prevailing westerly winds that dominate the weather in the temperate latitudes. Consequently, the storm slows down and changes direction— "recurves" in the language of the meteorologist. The path is that of the curved tracks shown in the figure.

The Coriolis force is largest at the poles and vanishes completely at the equator. This is why a Northern Hemisphere (counterclockwise) storm never crosses the equator to become a Southern Hemisphere (clockwise) one. In the few instances when hurricanes have been observed to approach the equator, they have been seen simply to fall apart. It is as if the winds didn't know which way to go without the Coriolis force to guide them.

What makes the Coriolis force unusual is that its existence depends on the observer's position. If you observe the earth from a satellite, there is no Coriolis force acting—everything is explainable perfectly well by reference to the action of the earth's rotation. It's only when you are on the earth itself that the force has to be invoked. It appears, then, that the way motion is described depends on the point of view from which it is observed. Because of this peculiarity, physicists often refer to the Coriolis force as "fictitious." That is a rather disturbing state of affairs, particularly if you retain confidence in classical physics, which says that there is somewhere a "correct" frame of reference to which all motion can be referred.

Having made this clear, I hasten to point out that although the two observers may differ in the words they use to describe the motion of the air in the storm, they are in perfect agreement as to the quantitative account of the motion. For example, if you ask them to predict how long it will take the block of air to get from point A' to point B' in Figure 7.4, they will both give you the same number in reply. What we have, then, is a situation in which observers occupying different frames of reference give different verbal descriptions of the events they see but arrive at the same mathematical equations. To put it another way, the events they see appear different, but the laws of nature governing those events that the observers derive in their respective frames are the same.

However abstract this discussion of hurricanes and Coriolis forces may seem, dealing as it does with phenomena well outside the range of everyday events, there is one example of a fictitious force that all of us can feel in our bones. I refer to the familiar experience of the centrifugal force.

We have all been in a car that has taken a sharp curve and felt ourselves pushed up against the door. If we think of this experience in the light of Newton's first law of motion, we probably reason as follows: I was sitting in the car minding my own business, so in Newton's terms I was a body at rest. Suddenly I was pushed toward the outside, which implies a change in my state of motion—hence, a force must have acted upon me. The force was pushing me away from the center of the circle around which the car was moving. I will therefore call that force centrifugal (center fleeing). I *know* the force was acting, because I could *feel* it.

All well and good, but now let us look at the same experience from the point of view of someone standing on the ground. This person sees you and the car moving along a straight path, then sees the car start to move into a curve. There is no new force acting on you—you continue to move in a straight line until prevented from doing so by the side of the car. So to an outside observer there is no force acting, at least at the start. Your motion toward the door is explained by the fact that you continue to move in a straight line while the car turns under you.

This is our old ambiguous situation about the storm: one observer sees a force acting, and another does not. As was true of Coriolis and his "force," so here we have the familiar centrifugal force labeled as "fictitious." In both cases, I want you to remember that when physicists use the word "fictitious," they do not mean imaginary. Your own experience tells you that the centrifugal force is as real as any other. You feel the force pushing you in the car just as surely as you feel the force of gravity pulling you down on the chair on which you are sitting.

Again, as was true of the Coriolis force, observers of the centrifugal force from different frames of reference describe it differently but agree on the basic laws that govern the motion. Yet another example of this phenomenon has had great historical significance.

Think for a moment about astronauts in orbit. We have all seen pictures of them floating around in their "weightless" environment. Why are they weightless? You often hear that it is because they are so far from the earth. But that can't be right. The force of gravity, as is well-known, depends on the distance between an object and the center of the earth. At the moment, you are about four thousand miles from the earth's center. Now, a typical shuttle in orbit goes only a little over a hundred miles farther away from that center. Surely one hundred miles out of four thousand is not enough to produce such a dramatic shift in apparent weight.

Actually, the weightlessness of astronauts is linked to the centrifugal force associated with their motion in orbit around the earth. From the point of view of the astronaut, several statements about forces are in order. First, since the astronaut floats about freely, the total force acting on him or her must be zero. If this were not so, astronauts would be accelerated by whatever forces were present until they hit the walls of their vessel—like the car passenger on a curve. That the total force is zero does not, however, mean that no forces are acting on the bodies. If the force of gravity on a body in orbit is almost the same as it would be on the surface of the earth, it acts inward, toward the center of the earth, but the centrifugal force of the shuttle moving in orbit acts in the opposite direction—outward and away from the earth. The only way the total force can be zero is for these two to be of equal magnitude. They then cancel and produce a net force of zero. And that is how "weightlessness" in orbital flight comes about. Gravity has not been lessened in any way, but the speed of the satellite is so great that the centrifugal force cancels out gravity.

Cancellation is a neat solution, but one problem remains. We have said that all observers must come to the same conclusion about the basic laws of physics in any situation involving fictitious forces. But how can an observer watching the satellite *and* the earth from outside the system find something that cancels the force of gravity on the astronaut?

The answer is that such an observer does not see gravity canceled at all. What that observer sees is an astronaut moving in a circular orbit around the earth. According to Newton's first law, this means that a force must be at work—otherwise, the astronaut would move in a straight line. From the point of view of the observer, the situation is like that shown in Figure 7.5. The astronaut, left alone, will move off in a straight line. But the force of gravity applies a "mid-course correction" and pulls him or her back. In this respect, the astronaut's motion does not differ from that of the wind blowing into a hurricane. As soon as the correction is applied, the astronaut moves off on a tangent again, is corrected again, and so on. The net result is a circular orbit in which the tendency of the astronaut to move off in a straight line is balanced by the fact that under influence of gravity he or she is actually falling toward the center of the earth. This interpretation of the orbit explains why you sometimes hear the term "free fall" applied to the astronaut's condition.

It was the realization that objects in orbit can be thought of as falling toward the earth that led Isaac Newton to the notion that the force of gravity is universal. He knew that it caused

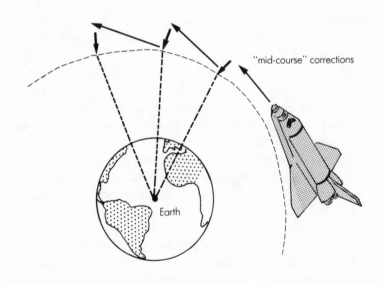

FIGURE 7.5

the apple to fall from the tree in his English orchard. By further reasoning—as we did above—he came to realize that the same force was capable of keeping the moon in orbit around the earth. For why limit our conclusions to an astronaut? The same argument will apply to anything circling the earth, including a large satellite such as the moon. In a very real sense, then, it was the contemplation of a fictitious force that led to the birth of modern science.

Still another fictitious force played a role in the development of the theory of relativity early in this century.* Like centrifugal force, this particular phenomenon is familiar to us all. We've all had the experience of feeling pressed back against the back of our seat when a car or an airplane starts to accelerate. Similarly, we have felt pushed down on the floor when an elevator starts to go up or of seeming to float when it starts down. All these feelings result from forces that act in one frame of reference but would not appear to be present if viewed from another. This, of course, is the signal that tells us we are dealing with a fictitious force.

Now suppose that you were standing on a scale in an elevator. When it started up, you would be pressed down on the floor, and your weight on the scale would register for a moment a higher figure than normal. Likewise, when you started down, you would appear to lose weight. But what we call weight is only the force exerted on us by gravity. In other words, the forces we feel in the elevator produce the same effects as gravity. It was this realization—that gravity itself may be a fictitious force—that led Einstein to formulate the general theory of relativity.

The central point of Einstein's theory is that while it is true that different observers will give different descriptions of what they see happening in a given event, they nonetheless will all agree on the basic laws of nature—that is, the equations that govern the event. Thus, while it might appear as if relativity led us into a kind of philosophical relativism in which each observer sees his or her own equally valid version of the uni-

---

*For a detailed account of this development, please see my book *The Unexpected Vista* (Scribners, 1983).

verse, this is not in fact the case. Each observer sees things from his or her point of view, but all agree that the universe is to be described by the same set of laws. What relativity does is to shift our attention from a description of events, which can vary from one observer to the next, to the laws that govern those events, which are truly universal.

EIGHT

When the Water Won't Boil

W E HAVE SEEN that the motive force for very small winds, such as those found in microbursts, and the motive force for the large-scale winds of the hurricane come from the same physical process—the energy release attendant on the conversion of water vapor into liquid water. That such a process plays a crucial role in weather phenomena is not surprising. After all, water vapor makes up a good portion of our atmosphere, and permutations and combinations involving water could be expected to have some sort of effect. What is surprising (to me, at least) is that after so many centuries of watching the weather, the study of the way that substances like water vapor shift from one form to another still occupies the central place in research. Indeed, it is still considered one of the most mysterious and most exciting fields of inquiry in modern science.

When water condenses from a vapor or evaporates from a

fluid, we say that it has undergone a change of phase. We normally speak of three phases of matter—solid, liquid, and gas. In general, any substance can exist in any of these phases provided the temperature is right. We know, for example, that steel, a solid at room temperature, can be converted to a liquid in a blast furnace. In laboratories, or in regions of very high temperature such as the surface of the sun, this liquid steel can be evaporated into a gas, just like water steaming away on your kitchen stove. Consequently, the study of phase transitions has a generality far beyond the question of how a storm system is powered.

Although it is not part of our everyday experience, there are many other examples of phase changes besides simple boiling and condensation. For example, when a lump of iron cools, it reaches a temperature at which it suddenly turns into a magnet. This transition is also a change of phase. Deep within the earth, minerals responding to the intense heat and pressure shift their constituent atoms around from one arrangement to another, releasing heat in the process. Just as evaporation and condensation of water provide the energy for the hurricane, the corresponding phase change in minerals within the earth may make some contribution to the overall temperature of our planet's interior.

All this suggests that we should now look at the structure of matter and see how such diverse phenomena can be understood in terms of some very simple physical models. This will lead us toward one of the most exciting fields of modern research—the investigation of the so-called critical phenomena and the development of a technique called the renormalization group. What this technique enables us to see is that regardless of the apparent differences between boiling water and magnetized iron, both are governed by processes that define the fundamental order of natural systems. Few better examples could be found of the underlying unity of natural phenomena than this similarity in the face of diversity. Finally, we shall come to the most interesting phase change of all—the one that occurred when the universe was only about 10 microseconds old and that set the course for the entire future evolution of the cosmos.

Let us start with a simple act—an ice cube is dropped into a soft drink on a hot summer afternoon. The molecules of water in the ice are locked together in rigid, Tinkertoylike arrangements by the forces that hold the atoms together. Push on one molecule and you move them all. This is the arrangement that gives a solid material its rigidity.

As the cube comes into contact with the drink, the ice starts to warm up. Collisions between the fast-moving atoms in the warm fluid and the slow-moving atoms in the ice effect an exchange of energy. The molecules in the liquid slow down (a process that we perceive as cooling), while the molecules in the ice speed up (a process that we perceive as warming). The net effect on the ice is this: each water molecule, though still attached to its place in the Tinkertoy lattice, starts to vibrate faster and faster as it absorbs the energy pouring into the ice cube. The faster vibration causes the molecules to wander farther and farther from their home base as the heating continues.

Eventually, the vibrations become so large that the molecules tear loose from their moorings and go floating off by themselves, a process we perceive as the melting of the ice cube or, in the language we should use here, as a change between the liquid and solid phase of water.* While this is going on, the temperature of the ice remains constant at 32° F. The process is analogous to the usual heating described earlier, except that now the energy flowing into the ice cube from the liquid is used to break the Tinkertoy bonds instead of raising the temperature. This explains why as long as there is ice in the drink, it stays cool. Only after the last chunks have melted will the drink start to warm up.

The change of phase from liquid to solid is thus fairly easy to visualize at the atomic or molecular level. The energy involved in the phase transition is that which is needed to break the bonds that hold the solid together. In the inverse process, by which a liquid freezes, the energy must be given out by the system, that is, removed, if the freezing is to proceed: you have to keep your refrigerator running if you want ice cubes. The

---

*The melting of water is actually a more complex process than indicated here. Whoever wants the full details can consult my book *Meditations at 10,000 Feet* (Scribners, 1986).

energy in the form of heat given off when the bonds form (or absorbed when the bonds break) is called the latent heat of fusion of the system. (The term "fusion" refers to the fusing of the molecules into a solid and has nothing to do with nuclear fusion reactions.) For water, the latent heat of fusion is about 80 calories per gram of material.

If we take the fluid left when the ice has melted and add heat, it will gradually warm up. The fluid phase of matter is characterized by molecules that are densely packed but not bound together very strongly. You can think of the molecular arrangements as being analogous to a bag filled with marbles —each marble able to slide more or less freely over its neighbors but remaining in contact with them nonetheless. As a fluid is heated, its "marbles" move more and more quickly. A few of the more energetic ones escape from the surface, a fact that explains why a drop of water evaporates even at room temperature. Eventually, a critical temperature is reached at which all the molecules in the fluid have enough energy to free them from the bonds that bind them to their neighbors. At that point, they fly off to form that collection of widely distant, freely moving objects we call a gas. This process is, of course, what we call boiling, or to use a more technical term, vaporization. As was the case with melting, the temperature of the fluid stays constant until the last molecules have escaped, for all the energy has gone into breaking the intermolecular bonds. The total energy needed to convert a liquid into a gas (and hence the total amount of energy released when a gas condenses into a liquid) is called the latent heat of vaporization.

The fact that the temperature of a boiling fluid remains constant no matter how much heat is added is a useful one. When you are cooking, for example, it is very convenient to have boiling water at 212° F. no matter what the stove setting. It means that anything you put into the water will be raised to this temperature and no higher. Anyone who has tried to make candy or worked with honey, where some other constant temperature has to be maintained, knows what a bother it is to keep fiddling with the stove and checking the thermometer to keep things even.

Experience with cooking also brings up another fact about phase transitions. The temperature at which a transition occurs is not a fixed and universal constant but varies with external conditions. For example, it is well-known that recipes that work well at sea level often produce unpalatable results when followed at high altitudes. I spend my summers at 5,000 feet in Red Lodge, Montana, and I've had ample opportunity to experience this effect firsthand. Even my borscht, justly famous in several states, was a disaster until I made a few adjustments. Likewise, when a civic group I am associated with put out a cookbook of ethnic recipes, we had to print a warning in the front so that tourists who tried to reproduce the dishes at lower elevations would know that they would have to experiment a bit to find the right temperature and timing.

What happens is that at higher altitudes the atmospheric pressure is lower than at sea level. Imagine the air pushing down on the water and restraining the flight of the molecules as they try to escape from the surface. The higher the pressure, the higher the temperature needed to get the molecules fairly launched—in other words, the higher the boiling point will be. Up in the mountains, water will boil at less than 212° F.

This dependence of the boiling point on pressure can also be demonstrated in the laboratory, where very high pressures can be generated. Quite high boiling points can be induced. At sea level, water boils at 212° F., but if you heat it in an environment where the pressure is more than two hundred times that of the normal atmosphere, the boiling point can get as high as 700 ° F. The increase is steady, that is, the higher the pressure, the higher the temperature.

This increase is steady until we reach a pressure of 217 atmospheres, at which point the boiling point is 705°. This is a very special set of values, for they define what is called the *critical point* for water: raise the pressure beyond the critical point and you can't get the water to boil no matter how high you push the temperature. In fact, above this point the distinction between fluid and gas seems to disappear.

The best way to understand the critical point is to imagine holding the water at 217 atmospheres and slowly raising the temperature toward 705°. On the way to this temperature, the water heats up exactly as water does in a pan on your stove. But as you approach the critical point, things begin to look strange. The water begins to break up into drops of liquid side by side with water vapor, a kind of blend of drops and bubbles. As we get closer and closer to the critical temperature, larger and larger bubbles and drops appear, although the smaller drops and bubbles remain. At the critical temperature itself, drops and bubbles ranging from the size of individual molecules to the size of the container are present. Beyond the critical point there is nothing but a single, misty undifferentiated phase that is both liquid and gas.

If this sort of thing happened only in water and other liquids, it would be a notable oddity but not a major subject for scientific research. But it turns out that critical points are found in many other systems in nature. The simplest occurs in the formation of a magnet from a lump of heated iron. Think of each atom of iron as being a tiny magnet, complete with its own north and south pole. At high temperatures, these little atomic magnets point every which way, and the result is that they cancel each other out; the lump of iron as a whole has no net magnetization. Put it near a nail and the nail won't move.

As you start to lower the temperature of the lump, nothing much happens until you get to around 1,418° F. (1,043° K.). At this temperature, the atoms interact with each other in such a way that all the atomic magnets begin to line up with each other and reinforce each other's magnetic field. Once this happens, the atoms are locked in place and remain in this arrangement as the temperature is lowered further. The result: the lump of iron is magnetized, and it will pick up a nail and do the other things we expect a magnet to do. The temperature that marks the dividing line between magnet and nonmagnet, 1,418°, is called the Curie temperature.

At first glance there may seem to be little connection between boiling water under high pressure and forming a magnet by cooling a lump of iron. But let us look in detail at what happens as the iron gets close to the Curie temperature.

A good way to visualize the transformation is to imagine the iron as broken up into little squares, as shown in Figure 8.1. In each square the atomic magnets combine to give a total net magnetism that, for the sake of simplicity, we assume to be either up (black in the figure) or down (white in the figure).

At temperatures above the Curie point, we get a situation

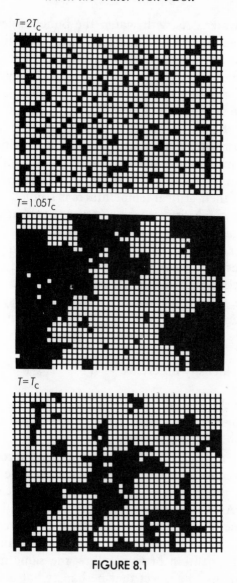

$T=2T_c$

$T=1.05T_c$

$T=T_c$

FIGURE 8.1

like the one shown on the top. The black-and-white squares are scattered at random throughout the sample, and the net effect is that there is no magnetization. On approaching the Curie point, the atomic magnets start to line up in little bunches, as shown in the middle. These bunches of up-and-down atomic magnets correspond to the droplets and bubbles we saw in water. As with water, the bunches get bigger and bigger, and at the Curie temperature itself the situation is that shown on the bottom: most of the groupings of atomic magnets point in one direction (up in this case), and only a few in the other. The net magnetization of the entire sample is "up"; the iron has turned itself into a magnet.

From the behavior of water and iron near their critical points, it is obvious that what is important in critical phenomena is the way that order is progressively established over larger and larger regions of a material. When the behavior of systems near their critical temperatures is studied in the laboratory, another similarity emerges. It turns out that the quantitative value that defines the material as a whole—density in the case of water, magnetization for the iron—depends on temperature in a very simple way. These values depend on the difference between the actual temperature and the critical temperature, or in other words on how far the system is from criticality. And this dependence follows a very simple law, which I write below for water.

$$\text{density difference} = ((T - T_C)/T_C)^\beta$$

By "density difference" we mean the difference between the density of the fluid at a given temperature T and the density it has at the critical temperature, T_C.

The magnetization of a lump of iron goes according to the same law, even to the value of the number β. The parameter β is called, in the jargon of the theoretical physicist, a critical parameter. As we shall see, many other systems in nature exhibit the same relation and have the same critical exponent.

That two such dissimilar processes as the boiling of water and the magnetization of iron follow the same mathematical formula leads us to suspect that perhaps what is important is not the details of the process taking place but the general property of systems that are becoming ordered. This suspicion is borne out by the results of the theory that has been developed to explain such critical phenomena.

The theory involves the forbidding term "renormalization group." The name arises because the theory was first developed to deal with a technical problem in the physics of elementary particles—something called the problem of renormalization. But you need not bother with renormalization. All you have to do is think about the things shown in Figure 8.2.

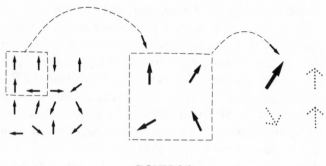

FIGURE 8.2

On the left we see a lump of iron with the atomic magnets aligned as they might be above the Curie temperature—all pointing in random directions. Now, dealing with all of them at once is a complex business. The trick of the renormalization group is to take the sixteen atomic magnets shown and replace each set of four by an "average" magnet, as shown in the center. Each "average" magnet represents the effects of the sum of the four real atoms in its square. But when you look at the figure in the center, you realize at once that this is just the same as the figure on the left. The only difference is that we now have a lattice made up of "average" magnets instead of real ones. The theory demands that the measurable quantities that characterize the system not change when we replace the true lattice by the averaged one. This requirement turns out to be enough to tell us how these "average" magnets interact with each other. Consequently, we can think of this new lattice as being identical with the old one. Once we do this, of course, the next step is obvious. We simply repeat the process, this time replacing the "average" magnets by the "average of the average" magnets, producing a new lattice as shown on the right. Clearly, this process can be repeated *ad infinitum*, with each averaging showing us the system on a different scale.

This operation is the heart of the renormalization-group procedure; what it does is to smear out the fluctuations in the real system. For example, in a magnet, the directions of the magnet can change from one atom to the next. In the jargon of physics we say that the fluctuations are on the scale of the atomic separation. When we consider the lattice made up of averaged spins (the central case in Figure 8.2), the spin can change from one average point to the other, but this represents two interatomic spacings. We say that for this case the fluctuations are on the scale of twice the spacing. Obviously, in the next step the scale of fluctuations is four times this spacing, then eight, and so on. At each step at which the procedure is applied, the scale of the fluctuations increases.

On this approach to the description of critical phenomena several interesting things can be said. The first is that it parallels what actually happens in nature, where the scale of the bunchings of atomic magnets or the drops and bubbles increases as we approach the critical temperature. The second point is that when the details of the theory are worked out (a process much too lengthy to go into here), the numerical value of the critical exponents can be calculated. In short, this seemingly simple way of looking at nature, in which we demand that the behavior of the system not change while we look at it at increasingly large scales, permits hard predictions that can be tested against experiment.

If this were the full extent of the power of the theory, it would still be enough to attract the attention of both physicists and philosophers. As it happens, there is even more to the story than this. By taking the theory as far as we can, we find ourselves considering an idea called "the hypothesis of critical-point universality." According to this hypothesis, the critical exponents, which tell us how the system behaves near the critical point, depend on only two things: the dimensions of the system and what physicists call the dimension of the order parameter. Let us look at these two characteristics separately.

Both the lump of iron and the heated water we have taken as examples exist in three dimensions, or to put it another way, each involves a physical system consisting of ordinary three-dimensional objects. In principle, of course, all ordinary physical systems exist in three dimensions, but for the purposes of the kind of analysis we are talking about, there are some that can be thought of as having a different number. A film of fluid on a surface, for example, can be considered as a two-dimensional system, and a long organic molecule, arranged like a chain of atoms, can be thought of as having only one dimension. Finally, and not so obviously, the world of the elementary particle, where the theory of relativity rules, must be thought of as a naturally occurring four-dimensional system, with the dimensions being the usual dimensions of space (three) plus time (one). The universality hypothesis tells us that the critical exponents for these kinds of systems will differ from each other but that systems within the same group will behave identically. But in all cases the general equation describing the approach to criticality given on page 112 will hold.

Here is a concrete example to pin this idea down. Imagine a hypothetical magnet in which all the atoms are confined to one plane. This would be a two-dimensional system. As it happens, this is one of the systems that can be solved exactly, and the result of the exact solution is that the critical exponent, β in our equation, that tells us how quickly the magnetization approaches its critical value is just $\frac{1}{8}$. This means that the difference between the magnetization at a given temperature, T, and its value at the Curie temperature is given by the equation

$$\text{difference} = ((T - T_C)/T_C)^{\frac{1}{8}}$$

For a real, three-dimensional system, however, the critical exponent has the value of .33, which is quite different from $\frac{1}{8}$ (.125). Thus, changing the dimension of the system changes its critical exponent.

The second quantity mentioned above, the "dimension of the order parameter," isn't nearly as bad as it sounds. In our examples (water and iron), what we discussed was density and magnetization as the system approaches the critical temperature. These quantities, in the jargon of physics, are an "order parameter." Just one number is enough to describe the order parameter in our two examples, so we say that it is one-dimensional. Most systems are of this type; a few are not, but do not confuse this one-dimensional order parameter with the one, two, three, or four dimensions of physical systems. Thus, when helium is cooled to within a few degrees of absolute zero, it undergoes a phase transition to what is called a superfluid phase—a state in which the liquid can flow without any friction—and it turns out that it requires two separate numbers to describe the order parameter in this transition. We then say that it has a two-dimensional order parameter.*

It would be hard to overemphasize the importance of the hypothesis of universality, for it shows that despite their seeming differences, many different systems in nature operate according to the same underlying principles; and further, that these principles have more to do with the way systems achieve order than with anything else. We saw water near the critical point and iron near the Curie temperature behaving alike, seemingly very different but brothers under the skin. Both systems are three-dimensional in character and have a one-dimensional order parameter. And as I intimated, other systems in nature possess these same properties, so we would expect them to have the same critical exponents and therefore the same behavior near their respective critical points.

One example of such a system is a mixture of oil and water. Under normal circumstances, these two do not mix. Not only does the proverb say so, but you can see it for yourself by letting a bottle of salad dressing sit until oil and water come apart and form separate layers. Nonetheless, you know that you can get a mixture of sorts by shaking the bottle. This yields a system in which little droplets of oil and water are mingled, although no droplet actually mixes with its neighbors. Now, if you raise the temperature, you will eventually get the oil and the water to mix. This is called the consolute point of the mixture. It is like the critical point and the Curie temperature in that it involves a phase change, from a two-fluid mixture to a single fluid. It is obviously a three-dimensional system. However, the order parameter, the dif-

*For the expert, these two numbers are the magnitude and phase of the superfluid amplitude.

ference in concentration of the two fluids, is something that can be expressed as a single number. Thus, the mixture of oil and water or any other two fluids near their consolute point exhibits the same behavior as a magnet or boiling water. To the physicist, the systems do not differ in any fundamental way.

A fourth typical system could be added to the list, for many alloys of metals, such as brass, undergo a phase transition from a state in which the atoms are arranged in a neatly ordered lattice to one in which they are all jumbled together. This is analogous to the oil-water situation, except that we are talking about concentrations of atoms instead of concentrations of fluid. No matter—the predictions according to theory are unambiguous. Alloys exist in three dimensions and have an order parameter definable with one number, so we know they behave near their critical point in the same way as all the others. They are just another system changing its state of order.

Finally, we can use our knowledge of phase transitions and critical behavior to talk about one of the most interesting systems of all—the early universe.* When the universe was a fraction of a second old, it consisted of a hot soup of all sorts of elementary particles. The most important of these from our point of view were the quarks, which we believe to be the basic constituents of matter. The familiar particles such as the protons and neutrons that make up the nuclei of atoms are now thought to be bound states of quarks. Early on, the universe contained a lot of free quarks, but they came together to form the particles that now make up the familiar universe.

At this point you should be able to recognize that the change from quarks to particles was just another transition between phases—more grist for the mill of the renormalization group. Of course, as was pointed out above, we are talking here of a four-dimensional system, so we must not expect the critical exponents to be the same for quarks as they are for water, but the principle of the theory is the same. As far as the order parameter goes, let me just say without explanation that it takes no fewer than thirty-two numbers to specify it for the hot quark soup. Nevertheless, when that soup condensed into or-

---

*You can learn about the details of how the universe evolved by looking at my book *The Moment of Creation* (Scribners, 1984).

dinary particles roughly 10 microseconds after the Big Bang, it approached its critical point by following the same laws as do all the other systems so far discussed.

That boiling water, heated iron, salad dressing, metal alloys, and the universe itself should all obey the same formula for critical points illustrates better than anything I could say the overwhelming beauty and elegance of our modern scientific view of the world.

NINE

Colors in the Sky

I N THE FIRST ESSAY in this book I spent a good deal of time talking about the colors in the sky at sunset, but I never touched on the part of the display that is often most striking—the clouds. The most spectacular sunsets are usually those in which clouds covering almost the entire sky slowly turn from a brilliant orange to a dull pink, then to gray and to blue as the darkness gathers. Obviously nothing happens to the constituents of the clouds in the time it takes the sun to go down, so why do they change color?

Let me cast this question in a slightly different form. We know that clouds are made from droplets of water, which is a clear, colorless fluid. Why, then, should they have any color at all? Why aren't they colorless like the water droplets of which they are made?

We can creep up on an answer to this question by noting (see

Fig. 9.1) that when we look at a cloud, we are seeing light that has been reflected from the cloud to our eye. The only exception to this rule is the case where the sun is directly behind a cloud. (I'll deal with that situation later.) For the moment, we simply note that the color of clouds depends in some way on the properties of light when it undergoes reflection.

When we discussed the blue color of the sky in chapter 1, we saw that when light encounters an air molecule, the blue is scattered more strongly than the red. It turns out that this is not what happens when the object encountered is the size of a water droplet in a cloud. In that case, all the different wavelengths of light are scattered in the same proportion: The droplet acts as a rough sort of mirror, sending out the same colors that come in.

During the day, as shown in Figure 9.1, the light that strikes the cloud comes directly from the sun and is therefore essentially white in color. Thus, the light that is reflected to our eye is white, as well, and the cloud takes on its familiar fleecy appearance. At sunset, on the other hand, the light from the sun

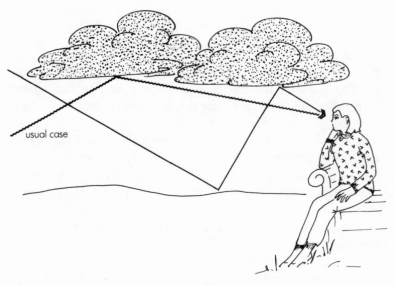

usual case

FIGURE 9.1

has to travel through a much longer path in the air, and the air molecules scatter out most of the blue light. The light that strikes the cloud and is reflected to the eye is therefore some shade of red. This accounts for the color of the clouds at sunset.

This explanation is borne out by a good deal of anecdotal evidence. It must happen sometimes that light from the sun travels along a path like the one on the right in Figure 9.1. It hits the ground, is reflected upward to the cloud, and then comes to the eye. In this case the light that strikes the cloud will be the color of the ground surface, and the cloud itself will take on that hue. In Scotland, for example, I have seen clouds take on a purple coloring as they pass over hillsides covered with blooming heather. The light that comes up from the ground is purple, and that color is faithfully reproduced in the light reflected from the cloud. I have been told that Eskimos navigating the ice floes of the Arctic Ocean use this property of the clouds to tell them where open water lies. They can see the difference in the light reflected from ice and open water and navigate their kayaks accordingly.

I must admit that I was a little dubious about this last report when I first heard it, but then a related phenomenon occurred to me—the reflection of city lights off low-hanging clouds. Sailors have long used the glow produced in this way to guide them to harbor, and Ernest Hemingway used the idea in *The Old Man and the Sea* when he has his hero guide his ship back to shore by using the lights of Havana reflected off the clouds. Using clouds as mirrors seems to be a fairly common technique, so I am no longer as skeptical of the story about the Eskimos as I once was.

The ability of large particles to scatter light of all wavelengths also appears in another, perhaps unexpected phenomenon. Some animals with white fur, such as polar bears, have no pigment in their hair. Instead, the hair shafts contain many tiny air bubbles, which play the same role as water droplets in clouds; they reflect all wavelengths equally. Thus the white of the polar bear and the white of the cloud are caused by the same physical process.

An even more unexpected connection between the color of

the sky and a familiar sight can be observed in the eyes of a newborn baby. As any parent can testify, human infants are born with blue eyes—eyes that only later assume their permanent color. What parent can forget that inquisitive period between six and twelve months when relatives look at the baby and try to guess what color the eyes will eventually be? Actually, babies are born with no pigment whatsoever in their eyes; the pupil contains many fine particles of a white, granulated substance whose grains are small enough to scatter blue light more strongly than red. Consequently, when white light falls on them, it is the blue part that is reflected back, and we see the eye as blue. Later, the permanent pigment develops in the pupil of the eye, and the color changes.*

Of course, the light that reaches our eye is not always the product of reflection. We have already seen one example of another process in what occurs when the sun is directly behind a cloud. (Please remember the warning on page vii and avoid looking directly at the sun under any circumstance.) On a heavily overcast day, you can usually tell where the sun is in the sky by looking for a whitish or yellowish spot in the clouds. Light from this spot is being transmitted through the clouds directly from the sun and is approximately the same color as the sun would be if no clouds were present. (The occasional yellow color is due to scattering of blue light by the air above the clouds.) We see, then, that the processes of reflection and transmission from water droplets in a cloud are similar in that the cloud will both transmit and reflect whatever colors fall on it.

This is not a universal property of materials. Think for a moment about the experience of being inside a chapel with stained-glass windows at night. This example is on my mind at the moment because I've just returned from a nighttime concert at the chapel of the University of Chicago, a Gothic revival building with enormous windows. From the inside of the building, the windows appeared to be a uniform dull gray. On a sunny day, however, they come alive with color.

*Anyone interested in reading about this and many other aspects of color should read Hazel Rossoti's marvelous book *Colour: Why the World Isn't Gray* (Princeton University Press, 1985).

The difference between these two situations is easy to understand, at least at a superficial level. At night, all the illumination comes from inside the building. Consequently, any light that comes to your eye must be reflected from the glass in the window. During the day, the light is coming from the sun, and what you see is light transmitted through the glass. So while a cloud reflects and transmits all wavelengths of light equally, stained glass is an example of material in which these two processes produce quite different results.

This leads us to another interesting question. How is it possible that the same set of atoms in the same material can respond so differently to light coming from two different directions? To understand how this comes to pass, we have to understand something about both the nature of light and the nature of atoms.

Light is a member of a class of objects known as waves, and as such is analogous to the waves you see on the surface of a lake. The essential feature of a wave is that its pattern of crests and troughs repeats as the wave moves by a given point. For our purposes, it is not important to know the exact nature of the light wave, but I will mention for the curious that it is made up of electric and magnetic fields that increase and decline in amplitude, just as the surface of a lake rises and falls as a wave moves along.

The quality we call color is related to the distance between crests in a light wave. As shown in Figure 9.2, this distance, known as the wavelength, is twice as long in red light as it is in blue; the other colors of the spectrum fall in between these two. The red and blue and the wavelengths between them are the only ones that will trigger a response in the human eye, but they constitute only a small fraction of the lightlike waves that exist in nature. Microwaves, X rays, infrared and ultraviolet radiation, and radio waves are all examples of waves similar in structure to light but with different wavelengths. We can detect all of these with suitable instruments, but only light is detected by sight.

When a light wave encounters an atom, the electric fields in the wave cause the electrons in the atom to move around and accelerate. It is this interaction that gives rise to the properties

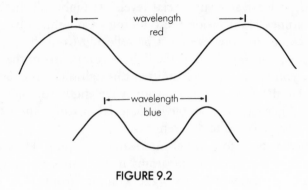

FIGURE 9.2

of color and light that we have discussed so far, as well as to a good many more still to be described.

In the nineteenth century, before the advent of quantum mechanics, people pictured the electrons as being tied to the atom by something like a flexible spring. This may seem like a strange way to picture an atom, especially to those familiar with the nucleus-plus-electrons-in-orbit image that we use today. Nevertheless, the visualization of an atom as a spring illustrates a very important aspect of the scientific method, one that is seldom noticed by scholars. When a scientist begins to investigate new areas of the physical world, he or she tries to integrate any new insights into former established principles. One way of doing this is to make a model of the new phenomena—to say "it behaves *as if* it were built like this." In this way, the strangeness of the new situation becomes more tractable, and if the model is a reasonable approximation to reality, real progress can be made.

The reason for this lies in the fact that the laws of physics are stated in mathematical equations. These equations constitute a kind of Rosetta stone or standard of reference that allows us to interpret the workings of nature in ways familiar to us. When we say that a model is a "reasonable approximation" of the truth, what we actually mean is that the equations that arise from the model are similar to those that later turn out to be correct. The symbols in the equation may be interpreted differently, but the basic form of the equations, and therefore the general predicted behavior of the system, will remain the same.

The model of the atom in which the electron is thought of as being attached to a spring is as good an example of this process as I know. No one in the nineteenth century seriously thought that there were little balls attached to springs inside the atom. (At least I hope no one did.) Nevertheless, the equation that describes the motion of the electron in such a model is basically the same as the equation arising from modern quantum mechanics. The interpretation changes, to be sure. For example, what was the *position* of the electron becomes the *probability* of finding it at a certain spot. But because the equations are the same, some pretty detailed processes have to be observed before it becomes clear that the spring model is only an approximation to reality. As we talk about the behavior of light and atoms in the next few chapters, I would like you to pause now and again and share with me the sense of wonder I feel when I see that the basic workings of nature are so simple and elegant that even a crude analogy can take us so far and teach us so much.

The central idea of the spring model is this: when a light wave encounters an atom, the electron finds itself subjected to two separate forces (see Fig. 9.3). It is pulled in one direction by the electric field of the light wave and pulled back by the

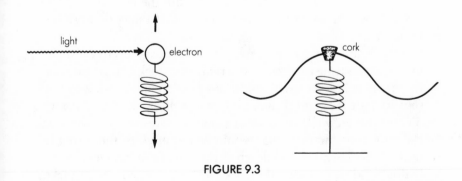

FIGURE 9.3

spring that attaches it to the nucleus. A useful analogy is shown on the right in the figure. A cork floats on the water, attached to the bottom by a spring that is just long enough so that it is neither stretched nor compressed when the water is at equilibrium level. If a wave should move by the cork, the ordinary force of buoyancy will pull it upward, as shown. As soon as it starts up, however, the spring will be stretched so that it, too, will exert a force opposing the upward motion. When a trough of the wave arrives, the cork will fall, the spring will compress, and an upward force will be exerted. No matter which way the cork moves, the spring tends to react in a way that counteracts the effects of the wave.

What happens to the cork when the wave arrives depends on two things: how closely spaced the crests of the waves are and how stiff the spring is. Suppose, for example, that the crests arrive so quickly after one another that the spring simply does not have time to stretch out between arrivals. The water will just wash over the cork, and the cork itself will never move very far from its normal position. At the other extreme, there can be a situation where the crests of the wave are so far apart that the spring has plenty of time to adjust. In that case the cork would bob slowly up and down, following the changing water level.

The point of this example is that in neither case does the cork move very fast. In the language of physics, we would say that the cork never acquires much energy from the wave. It follows that the energy of the wave after it has encountered the cork is always close to what it was before the encounter. The wave proceeds on its way pretty much as if the cork were not there at all.

This is not always the case. If the successive crests of the wave arrive at just the right intervals, the cork can be boosted to larger and larger oscillations, much as a child's swing can be sent to a great height if the pushes are well timed. For the cork on the spring, well timed means that the crests must arrive at the same time intervals that would be required for the spring to bounce the cork up and down if there were no water present. If this condition is met, the cork can be set moving quite fast, which means that it must absorb a lot of energy from the wave, and the wave leaving the cork will be diminished from what it was coming in.

The final picture of the interaction between the wave and the cork is quite simple. When the separation between crests is very different from that needed to allow the cork to bob up and down at its natural frequency, only a small amount of energy will be transferred from the wave to the cork, and such a wave would be able to travel for a long way through an array of corks. If on the contrary the crests arrive at just the right intervals, the wave will lose a great deal of energy to the cork and travel only a short distance through the array.

The wave that we call light will move an electron around in an atom just as the water wave moved the cork. If the distance between crests—that is, the wavelength—of the light is just right, then as the wave proceeds through the material and encounters one atom after another, it will gradually be attenuated and after a time simply disappear—all of its energy will have been transferred to the atoms.

But the wavelength of the light, as we saw, corresponds to its color. Consequently, the wave and electron picture just described tells us that a given electron in an atom will absorb certain colors from the light that hits it and allow other colors to pass on largely unaffected. White light may fall on one side of a piece of material, but if the atoms within the material are such that they absorb everything except light of a certain wavelength, what is seen by someone on the other side of the piece of material will be only the color that has not been absorbed.

This explains part of the puzzle of the stained glass. Transmitted light seen through such glass depends not only on the light coming in but on which components of that light are absorbed by the atoms. What finally comes through to the other side is what is left when all the atoms have had their way with the crests and the troughs of the light.

To understand the rest of the puzzle, we have to think about what happens to the energy after it has passed from the wave to the electron. Ordinary atoms can be quite complex things, with many electrons circling each nucleus. When one of these electrons acquires some extra energy, a number of things can happen. For example, the energy of that single electron can be shared with the atom as a whole. Most commonly, the effect of this transfer is to cause the entire atom to move more quickly, and we say that the energy of the incoming light has been converted into heating up the material. The light disappears, and the temperature goes up. From our point of view, this process (quite common in nature) represents a sort of dead end, for after it occurs, there is no more light to think about.

Alternatively, the single electron that has been set into rapid oscillations can take the energy it has been given by the incoming light wave and put it back into another light wave, this one emanating outward from the atom like the ripples that result from throwing a rock into a still pond. The color of this outgoing wave can be the same as that of the incoming light (if only the absorbing electron does the radiating) or different (if some of the other electrons share in the absorbed energy). This process is sketched in Figure 9.4, below. First the light is absorbed by an electron; then the energy is radiated. The net effect is that a light wave moving uniformly to the right in the figure has been converted to an outgoing wave centered on the individual absorbing atom.

As the wave progresses through the material, then, more and more atoms start emitting these secondary waves, as shown in Figure 9.5. At any point in the body of the material, secondary waves from many atoms come together. In most cases, the results cancel one another. If there were a charged particle at

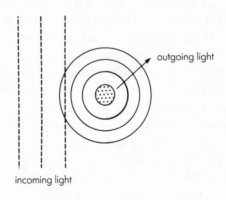

outgoing light

incoming light

FIGURE 9.4

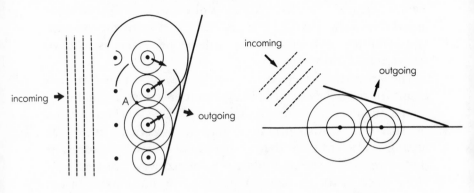

FIGURE 9.5

A, each wave would arrive and give it a different signal—one says to move up the full amount, another to move down, a third says not to move at all, and so on. The net effect of all of this is that the particle doesn't move at all, and the observer would say that the net effect is that of a "wash item" in a budget. There are only two exceptions to this general state of affairs, as shown in Figure 9.5, above. One of them occurs at certain points in the forward direction, as shown on the left. At these points the secondary waves from all the atoms and what is left of the incoming wave arrive together—if the crest of one appears, so does the crest of another. Note that the part of the incoming wave that has not been absorbed can be thought of as just one more wave arriving among many—one more wave whose presence must be taken into account.

Any particle along this line, then, will experience a large force as all of these waves act in concert. As a result, the wave that entered the material now moves in a new direction—a direction defined by the perpendicular to the line along which this reinforcement occurred. This is the explanation of the phenomenon of refraction discussed in chapter 1—a phenomenon, you will recall, that is responsible for many of the strange optical effects seen at sunset, from "corners" on the sun to the green flash.

The second exception to the general rule about waves

"washing out" is in the backward direction, as shown on the right in Figure 9.5. There will be a direction in which secondary wavelets emitted by electrons in the surface of the material will reinforce each other. This will be perceived as a wave reflected back from the surface.

The properties of electrons and light waves, therefore, account for the behavior of light. When it encounters a material, the incoming beam splits into two parts. One is reflected from the surface, the other penetrates into the material, traveling at an angle different from that of the original wave. We speak of these two as the reflected and the refracted wave, respectively. How much of the energy of the original beam remains in the form of light waves and how much is converted into heat depends on how the electrons in the material are arranged and how they react to energy once it is absorbed from the wave. We will go into this question in more detail in the next chapter, but for the moment we simply note that there is a wide range of possibilities here, each resulting from a different arrangement of the electrons. A piece of black metal on a wood stove, for example, will absorb all of the light that hits it, reflecting very little, transmitting none, and converting almost everything into heat. A sheet of window glass, on the other hand, will absorb almost none of the energy of the wave, which will be transferred to the refracted wave. This wave, when it reemerges from the glass, will travel to our eye and allow us to see what is on the other side of the glass. In general, very little of the energy is transferred to the reflected wave, which is therefore usually quite weak. This is why images reflected in windows generally appear darker and less vivid than the real thing.

In the stained glass that started these ruminations, the electrons are so arranged that all colors except one are absorbed and converted into heat, while that privileged color is refracted and transmitted through the glass. As with ordinary window glass, little energy goes into the reflected wave, which explains why the windows look so dark and lifeless when viewed from the inside. In the end, then, all color depends on how electrons in a material absorb and reradiate the energy of incoming light.

Reradiation deserves somewhat more discussion, if only because we make use of it so often in our daily lives. According to the theory that governs the behavior of electrical objects, whenever a charged particle like an electron is accelerated, it will convert some of its energy of motion into radiation. If the electron happens to be in an atom, this radiation, as we have seen, will be in the form of light. If the electron happens to be the wires of a radio or TV transmitting antenna, the radiation emitted will have wavelengths of many feet or even miles, and then we say it is in the form of radio waves. When these waves, after traveling through the air, encounter the electrons in the wire of your television or radio antenna, they cause these electrons to move, as well. The motion in the antenna constitutes an electrical current, which the receiving device, whether radio or TV, converts into the visual or audio signal that you see or hear. So the next time you sit down to listen to your favorite program, you might spare a moment for the thought that the natural phenomena that allow you to do so are exactly the same as those that make stained-glass windows or clouds at sunset such beautiful things to behold.

TEN

Roses Are Red, but What about Geraniums?

I T WAS A DISAPPOINTMENT I don't think I'll ever forget. I was perhaps six or seven, and it was my first outing on that particular stretch of beach. As I strolled about, I found and pocketed a collection of the most beautiful gemlike stones I had ever seen. Unlike their counterparts farther inland, these wave-washed pebbles possessed deep, lustrous colors. Imagine my surprise when, at the end of the day, I went to my room to survey my treasures and found that I had a pocketful of ordinary, bland, dull rocks. Somehow, in drying off, they had lost their beauty. It was years before I learned how such a dramatic change of color could happen.

This experience touches on a very old question in natural philosophy: what is the nature of color? This, in turn, is part of a still larger question: what is the nature of sight and seeing?

The standard answer in ancient times was that some sort of

rays emanated from the human eye and made contact with the object in sight. This theory rested on an analogy between the senses of touch and sight. We touch things by reaching out and coming into close physical contact with them, and according to the theory we see things in the same way. The eye must emit rays that act like grappling hooks; they reach out to the thing being viewed and bring it into sight. Greek thinkers such as Pythagoras and Aristotle spoke of "invisible fire" being emitted by the eye, and this was still the view taught during the Middle Ages in the universities of Europe. The objections of the great tenth-century Arab scientist Alhazen, who pointed out that this theory could not be right because you can see the sun through closed eyelids, made no headway against Aristotelian orthodoxy. Not until well into the seventeenth century did something like our modern theory of vision begin to take shape.

The debate on the nature of color followed a somewhat different path. As we shall see, perceiving color involves three quite different processes. First, there has to be interaction between light waves and atoms of the type discussed in the previous chapter. This interaction produces a light wave that falls on the eye. The production of this light wave, which acts as the stimulus to the human sensory system, may be called the physical part of seeing color. Once the light wave enters the eye, a complicated series of optical and chemical reactions takes place. The net effect of these reactions is an electrical impulse that travels along the optic nerve to the brain. This second stage of seeing a color we shall call the physiological part of color vision. Finally, once the signal reaches the brain, it is interpreted in terms of a complex matrix of information possessed by the person doing the seeing. Contrary to what you might suppose, the color you see does not depend solely on the wavelength of the light that strikes your eye but on other things in the visual field and in the mind of the viewer. This third component is the psychological part of color perception.

That seeing colors should be such a complex process is perhaps not particularly surprising—after all, what is simple these days? We are prepared for the worst; but during the debate over color that continued for centuries, this tolerant expectation was little in evidence. Physicists who studied color liked to feel that it was only necessary to unravel the mystery of the light waves; *that* was what color really meant. Physiologists, and later psychologists, made similarly absolute claims for their special fields of knowledge. Only recently, in the mid-twentieth century, have scientists come to understand that seeing colors involves a complex blending of all three processes.

You can see for yourself why that is so if you will reflect on a few familiar situations. When you dine by candlelight, the tablecloth looks white. This is true even though the light given off by the candle and subsequently reflected to your eye is yellow. If you measured its wavelength or ran it through a prism, you could obtain clear proof of this fact. How, then, does the tablecloth come to appear white even though the light coming from it is yellow? Obviously, the fact that we know the tablecloth is "really white" influences what we see. The psychological component of color is at work.

At the same time, knowledge (or psychology) cannot be the only factor. Any shopper knows that the color of a new suit or shirt seen under a fluorescent light in the store looks different from what it does in sunlight. A wise shopper takes the garment to the door or window. Clearly, the different tint has to do with the different nature of the light striking and being reflected from the cloth in each case; it is independent of the state of mind of the observer. What better evidence that the color we see depends on the physics of light waves?

Finally, the evidence for a physiological component is manifest if we think about such a common condition as color blindness. Persons who possess perfect eyesight in every other way can lack the ability to see certain colors. A famous historical example of this defect is that of the nineteenth-century Scottish chemist John Dalton, the man who formulated the first modern version of the atomic theory. He wrote that when he looked at geraniums—flowers his friends all described as pink—he saw something that was sky blue by day and red by candlelight. His name has been attached to the peculiarity—Daltonism. A modern physician would say that Dalton's retina lacked the red-sensitive pigment normally found in the eye. For our purpose, we simply note that the existence of color blindness establishes the fact that color vision depends in part on the physiology of the eye.

Having ascertained these three factors, we can go on to examine each separately. In the last chapter we saw that the interaction of light with atoms is governed by the behavior of electrons in the atoms and particularly by the way in which the electrons are constrained by the forces connecting them to the nucleus. I suggested that we could think of this force as being exerted by a spring linking the two. For the subject of that chapter, this level of complexity was sufficient. To explain color, we have to look into the behavior of the electron a little more deeply.

In most atoms of the kind under discussion, there are many electrons in a cloud around the nucleus. In addition to the electrical force exerted by the nucleus, each electron feels itself being repelled by each of its brothers. In effect, the atom can be thought of as a web of forces that shift and change as the electrons move about their orbits. One way of picturing this web is to imagine each electron as being held to the nucleus by a strong spring and to the other electrons by a mesh of lighter, weaker springs. The motion of each electron is thus primarily determined by its relation to the nucleus, but the details of the motion are affected by the presence of other electrons. This situation is shown on the top of Figure 10.1.

The other electrons in the web need not be in the same atom as the one we wish to study. In solids and liquids, the atoms are packed together cheek by jowl, as shown on the bottom of Figure 10.1. It would not be at all unusual for one electron to be closer to another electron in a neighboring atom than to an electron in its own atom. Thus, electrons are subjected to forces exerted by neighboring atoms as well as to the "domestic" ones already described. If these new forces are imagined as weak springs, then we have to picture each electron as bound into the material by a large assortment of such devices. Some springs attach it to other electrons in its own atom, others to electrons and nuclei in other atoms. It is, in fact, this complex web of interactions that holds the material together and allows it to keep its shape when other forces (such as gravity) are applied from outside.

The motion of any given electron, then, will depend on the particulars of the web in which it finds itself, or to put it another way, on the location of the electrons in its own and sur-

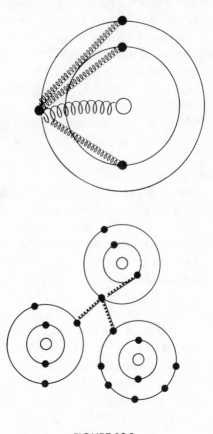

FIGURE 10.1

rounding atoms. We know from an earlier discussion that the way a material absorbs and reemits light depends on the way that electrons move when they are illuminated by a light wave. Thus, anything that affects the web of forces will also affect the response of a material to light. Since color is one example of such a response, we should not be surprised that seemingly minor changes in the way atoms are arranged can have profound effects on the colors we see when we look at objects. Any of these changes causes a different response to incoming light. In a nutshell, that is why so many different processes can affect color.

Think back to my gemlike pebbles on the beach. We know that light striking a surface and upsetting the electrons will be partly reflected and partly refracted into the interior of the material. The stone is opaque, of course, so refracted light does not penetrate very far into it. But it does travel far enough to encounter many of the atoms that compose the stone. Some wavelengths of this refracted light are absorbed, while others are sent back out. It is the waves that have penetrated the surface and then come back to the eye that give the stone its characteristic colors, for it is these waves from which all but a few wavelengths of light have been removed.

The brightness of the colors depends on the amount of the original light that gets past the surface of the material and undergoes absorption in the interior. Two possible situations are shown in Figure 10.2. On the left, most of the light is reflected, because the irregularities of the surface produce a uniform background of scattered light. Against this background, the relatively weak refracted beam that carries the colors will look washed out, and the colors of the object will appear dull and subdued.

On the right, you see the opposite case. A relatively weak reflection from the surface and a strong beam from the interior. What comes to your eye will be strongly influenced by the atoms in the interior of the material and will appear brightly colored. In short, the brightness of the color we per-

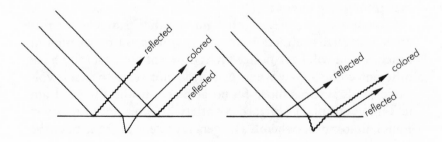

FIGURE 10.2

ceive when we look at an object depends on the relative strengths of the reflected and refracted beams.

These relative strengths, in turn, depend on the interaction of the incoming light with electrons in the surface and, in particular, on the way those electrons move in response to that light. If the web of forces favors one type of motion, reflection will be strong; if it favors another, refraction will be favored. So the riddle Why do the beach pebbles change color? comes down to this: why do the electrons in the surface act differently when the stone is wet than they do when it is dry?

Having learned about the web of forces, we are now in a position to answer the question. When the stone is wet, electrons on the surface find themselves flanked on one side with water molecules. These molecules produce one web of forces. When the surface is dry, the electrons find on one of their sides only an occasional oxygen or nitrogen molecule to contend with. The electrons move among a quite different force. Calculations show that the first of these situations favors refraction, the latter reflection.*

To recapitulate: when you pick up a brightly colored rock at the beach, the water molecules at the surface affect the surface electrons in such a way that most of the light penetrates into the rock and comes out again, bearing the imprint of the atoms inside; the stone appears strongly colored. If you put the pebble in the sun and watch it dry, you will see the color fade and become washed out. What is happening is that the surface layer of water is evaporating and the electrons, responding to the new environment, reflect more of the light and allow less to penetrate to the interior.

Common experience supplies many other examples of this reflection versus refraction effect. If you spend much time at beaches, you will have noticed that different kinds of sand have different colors, even when dry. I do not refer to black volcanic sands such as those found at places in the Pacific; I am talking about plain old garden-variety brown sand of the type found almost everywhere. The general rule is this: the finer the

---

*A scientist will be aware that this result comes about because the index of refraction of water is higher than that of air and is thus closer to the index of refraction of the material in the rock.

sand, the lighter the color. A sand of coarse grain has a defi-nite brown color, even high up on the beach where it is dry, whereas a very fine sand may be almost white, even though it is made of the same stuff as its coarser neighbor. How can we understand this difference?

Sand grains are small and have a relatively high proportion of their atoms on the surface instead of the interior. The finer the grains, the truer this is. As the grains get smaller, we would expect the amount of reflection to increase compared to the amount of light refracted from the interior. This has nothing to do with changes in the web of forces in the electrons, of course; it depends on the different ratios of surface to volume in the different grains.

Since the fine grains have more surface relative to their vol-ume, they will reflect relatively more white light, thus showing a more diffuse background against which any colored light that may be present is seen. Thus, the finer they are, the whiter they appear. By the same token, the larger grains, having a smaller surface area relative to their volume, will show a less diffuse background and will appear darker. There is no funda-mental difference between the white sand of the Caribbean beaches and the coarse sand of Maine, even though they look quite different.

If you come upon a traffic accident you can observe this same transition in appearance from coarse to fine-grained ma-terial. You will see small pieces of colored glass at the site of the collision and notice how repeated crushings by passing cars reduce them to a white powder. The reason for the change of colors in the glass is the same as it was for the sand. The initial impact of the cars produced large chunks that had a large vol-ume compared to their surface area. At a busy intersection the grinding down of these chunks to a size where more light is scattered from the surface than from the interior takes only a few days or hours, whereas it takes thousands of years for the sand of a beach. The end product is the same, however. With-out any change in chemical composition, the color of the mate-rial is changed.

These examples enable us to talk about further aspects of color in very general terms; but if we are interested in the particular and ask, for instance, why the sand is brown and the glass red, we must start looking at individual atoms.

It is surprising how much the nature of neighboring atoms can affect the way a given atom responds to light. To take a case, the brown color in the Maine sand is due to the presence of occasional iron atoms in the crystal structure of the rocks from which the sand grains were made. These iron atoms are impurities in the structure—in a perfect crystal they would not be present: pure quartz is colorless. Contamination from trace elements when rocks are formed is usual, so common atoms such as iron usually creep in. In brown rocks, the combined effect of the iron impurities and the silicon and oxygen atoms that make up the bulk of the structure produces a web of forces that impart to the material a brownish, reddish, or yellowish color in the light with which it interacts.

The sensitivity of electrons to the web of forces can be appreciated by noting that the same iron atom whose effects give sand its brown color will, if placed in a slightly different environment, produce the greenish color of pale jade. In the same way, slight admixtures of chromium atoms can produce either the red of the ruby or the green of the emerald and the dark jade—all depending on the details of the web into which these atoms are placed and their effect upon it. If sulphur occurs in conjunction with metal impurities, you may get a web that absorbs all wavelengths of light equally well. The result is a total absence of color, or black. It is the presence of sulphur in the air that causes silver to tarnish.

When we pass from natural to artificial colors, the situation becomes even more complex. Paint is not a uniformly colored fluid, as anybody knows who has had to mix a can of paint that has been sitting for a long time. It is made up of two components: one is a clear liquid like water or oil, the other a sludgy, colored material that sinks to the bottom of the can. In a well-mixed paint, the colored particles are in suspension in the fluid, and the size of these particles is of crucial importance. If they are much smaller than the wavelength of visible light, then we know from chapter 1 that they will scatter blue light better than any other, and the paint will take on a bluish cast regardless of the intrinsic color of the particles. If the particles are too large, on the other hand, they will not stay in suspension very long. In most modern paint, the pigments are ground down to the point where the dimensions of the particles are roughly the same as the wavelength of visible light.

After paint has been applied, the liquid base evaporates, leaving a colored coating behind. The only real requirements of the pigments used are that they form a coating with good mechanical properties—that they not blister or crumble, for example—and that they not undergo chemical changes under the action of light or weather. One occasionally sees large fields where paint companies test their products for these properties. They use the simplest experimental technique: different materials are painted with the new products and left out in the sun and rain for months, perhaps years, at a time. The paints that survive the test are then marketed; the rest go back to the laboratory. These testing areas are bright spots of color along a highway or in a city and are unmistakable to the passerby.

Another type of artificial coloring—dye—differs from paint, although it yields much the same result. Instead of carrying color in fine grains, the working element in a dye is a single large molecule. Such molecules are dissolved in a liquid (usually water) into which the fabric to be colored is dipped. As the fibers of the fabric absorb the water, they expand and start to push apart, opening up microscopic holes into which the fluid and its molecular cargo can flow. When the cloth is dried, the water evaporates, leaving behind the molecules, which, because of their own peculiar web of forces, return a particular color when light hits them.

Unlike the making of paints, the production of a dye does not call for finding something mechanically strong but finding something that is "fast," that is, that will stay in the cloth. Traditional natural dyes were made from things like molluscs or ground beetle shells, whose properties were known from long centuries of use. When in the nineteenth century the synthetic dye industry started in Germany, finding ways of making the new dyes as permanent as the natural ones turned out to be a difficult undertaking indeed. Almost fifty years passed before truly dependable synthetic dyes were available for commercial use. Today, all dyes that you are likely to encounter are synthetic.

The development of the large-scale manufacture of paints

and dyes, together with the popularity of photography, led to a great deal of scientific interest in the physical nature of colored light. One of the great pioneers in this field was the Scottish physicist James Clerk Maxwell, who is better known as the founder of the modern theory of electromagnetism. In 1860, Maxwell produced the first color photograph (which I understand is still on display in Cambridge, England). He also worked out the modern tristimulus theory of color. He found that any color can be produced by mixing light of three different colors together. The choice of these so-called primary colors is arbitrary, but they are customarily taken to be red, blue, and green. He demonstrated his ideas by the use of a Maxwell wheel, shown in Figure 10.3. The three primary colors are placed on the disk in different proportions, as shown, and then the disk is spun rapidly. The result is that the eye, unable to follow the rotation, adds the colors together in proportion to the amount of each received and perceives a new and different color in the disk.

The need to standardize this principle of color mixing was met in the 1920s by a team of British researchers. Using large groups of people with normal eyesight, they worked out the

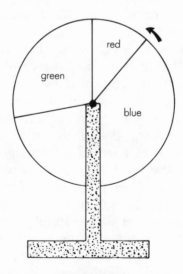

FIGURE 10.3

equivalence between wavelengths of light and the way the eye perceives a given mixture of the three primary colors. To each color in the spectrum they were able to assign fixed proportions of red, green, and blue that would, when processed by the human eye, produce the same sensation as the original single wavelength. For example, light whose wavelength is 580 nm,* something we would say was reddish-orange, will be perceived to be identical to light made up of a mixture of red, green, and blue in the ratio 916:870:1.7. In 1931 the International Commission on Illumination adopted these types of ratios as the standards for the definition of color.

With this development the first requirement for an understanding of color—an unambiguous definition of the properties of the wave that comes to the eye—was met. The physical aspects of color vision, both the way color originates and the way it is characterized, were now well understood. Work on the second part of the question, the element of physiology, has gone on throughout the nineteenth and twentieth centuries, so that we also have a pretty good notion of how the eye translates a stimulus into a nerve impulse on its way to the brain.

When light enters the eye, it is focused on the retina at the back of the eyeball. There it encounters two sorts of light-sensitive cells called the rods and the cones. These names have nothing to do with function, only with the shape of the cells as seen under a microscope. In effect, the rods and the cones equip the back of the eye with two different sorts of television cameras. The rods are very sensitive (i.e., they respond to very small amounts of incoming light), but they do not respond to color—they are a black-and-white camera. It is the rods that permit seeing in dim light or in the dark. When the incoming light gets too bright, the rods switch off, and the cones come into play.

The cones give us color vision. They contain large molecules that absorb incoming light and act as the first step in the process that converts the energy of that light into a nerve impulse.

---

*A nanometer (nm) is a unit of length equivalent to one billionth of a meter, or about one-tenth the distance across a typical atom. It is now, by convention, used in scientific work dealing with the wavelength of all radiation, including light.

Cones occur in three different types, each carrying a slightly different type of molecule. The web of forces acting on the electrons in each molecule is such that the three kinds of cones are sensitive each to a different wavelength of light. One is most efficient at absorbing blue light, another at absorbing green, and the third at absorbing red. Obviously, Maxwell's three-color theory of color vision has a firm foundation in the physiology and chemistry of the eye.

Like most physicists, I have always had a particularly naive view of color vision. I took it for granted that once the physics of light and the chemistry of the eye had been worked out, there was nothing more to be said. I am indebted to my friend and colleague at the University of Virginia, Frank Hereford, for showing me the error of my ways. After ten years as president of the university, Frank came back to the physics department ready to find a good research project and dig into it. He chose color vision as a challenge and got busy. One day in his office he showed me some things he had made out of colored bits of paper and plastic that convinced me that there was a great deal more to color vision than I had thought.

Looking at a sheet on which colored scraps had been pasted in a seemingly haphazard pattern, I quickly realized that the color perceived is strongly influenced not only by the light coming from a particular source, but also by what is being received from neighboring spots, as well. I was, moreover, given a chance to look into an apparatus where a screen separated what was seen by one eye from what was seen by the other. Imagine my surprise when I found that I could make a particular patch, seen with one eye, "change color" simply by opening and closing the other eye! I came away convinced that the mind played a major role in color vision, just as physics and physiology do.

After looking into the question a little more, I found that the surprising things I had seen were well known to scholars and that practical men knew about the psychological aspect of color vision as long ago as 1824. In that year, Michel-Auguste Chevreul told the weavers of tapestries in France that they should be careful about putting certain colors next to each other in their works, because the colored patches would appear to fade near their boundaries.

The problem that concerned tapestry makers is a special case of a well-studied phenomenon that has to do with the appearance of sharp boundaries between areas of different colors. The effect is most striking when the colors are complementary. If one area is yellow and the other blue, the color near the boundary will look much more pale than the color in the main bodies. Nothing that we know about the structure of the eye suggests a reason why this should happen. Light from the blue patch should be striking one region of the retina, light from the yellow patch another, and there should be a sharp dividing line between the two. It appears that somewhere in the "wiring" of the system there is a way for each cone to know what its neighbors are up to. The effect is that hitting one cone with blue and its neighbor with yellow produces the same response as if both had been hit with white—the two colors are mixed together *after* they have been detected in the eye.

The explanation for our seeing a "color" that isn't there is probably rather mundane; perhaps it is due to the way the nerves in the eye are connected with each other. And if this were the only type of evidence for a psychological dimension to color vision, it could probably be argued that we were just playing with words—that quirks in the way the nerves in the retina are connected are really a part of the physiology of the eye. But there is a much more dramatic (though less commonly seen) demonstration of the presence of "psychology."

I saw this demonstration given by Edwin Land, the inventor of the Polaroid camera. He had prepared two slides, both photographs in black and white of the same scene. The only difference between the two slides was that one had been taken through a red filter, the other through a green. He then set up an ordinary white screen and two slide projectors, one with a red filter in front of the bulb, the other equipped with the usual white bulb. He put the "red" slide in the first projector, the "green" slide in the other, and focused both on the screen. The resulting picture had all sorts of colors in it—blues, yellows, oranges. These colors appeared on the screen even though the wavelengths of light corresponding to those colors were absent from the light striking the eye. Obviously, the mind was doing something to produce colors where none really existed. This demonstration was particularly effective because it was done in front of an audience of physicists who, like myself, thought there was a simple one-to-one correspondence between the wavelength of light coming to the eye and the color perceived.

Unlike the appearance of neighboring colors in the tapestry, Land's demonstration cannot be brushed aside as an extension of physiology. Some of the colors were like the white in the tablecloth mentioned on page 134—they were the result of the observer's expectation that certain objects would take on certain colors. It is well-known, for example, that someone shown a picture of a brick and a leaf, both the same shade of gray, will see the leaf as being a greener shade of gray than the brick. Other colors in Land's demonstration may have come from the kind of mixing that we discussed above, and still others from processes we still don't understand. In any case, Land certainly convinced a roomful of physicists that there is much more to color vision than the physics of light and the chemistry of the eye.

What I find fascinating in this story is that a simple everyday experience like seeing the color of a flower carries within it so much basic science and, in the end, shows us that whatever the external world may do, the mind has the ability to put its own unique stamp on what it receives.

ELEVEN

The Scale of Things, or Why You Can't Get a Suntan through a Window

H AVE YOU EVER NOTICED that when you sit next to a window on a summer day you never get a tan, no matter how hot and uncomfortable you get? You know that if you had been sitting outside on the lawn, you would have been burned to a crisp.

When you think about this contrast for a while, you must admit that it is puzzling. As we have shown in the last two chapters, that glass is transparent means that the electrons in it cannot absorb energy from the light that strikes it. Furthermore, whatever it is that causes our skin to tan or burn must be part of the sunlight. How can the same set of electrons in the glass fail to absorb the light we see and at the same time absorb or reflect whatever light brings with it?

The answer to this question is twofold. One part depends on the nature of sunlight, the other on the way the electrons are locked into the atomic structure of the glass. The sun, powered by fusion reactions deep in its core, has a surface temperature of about 6,000° C. Anything as hot as this gives off radiation of many different wavelengths. Figure 11.1 is a sketch of the amounts of radiation given off by the sun. Those corresponding to visible light are marked by the two vertical lines. A glance at the figure shows that in addition to the wavelengths that correspond to the colors from red to blue—the wavelengths discussed so far—the sun also emits waves of longer length than red and shorter than blue. The former is called infrared radiation, the latter, ultraviolet.

It is the ultraviolet radiation that is relevant to our conundrum. The general rule is that the shorter the wavelength, the more energy the wave has. Thus, blue light is more energetic than red; ultraviolet, more energetic than blue. Most of the ultraviolet light that strikes the upper atmosphere is absorbed by atoms in the ozone layer, and only a relatively small amount penetrates to the surface of the earth. This is a good thing, because ultraviolet radiation in large doses is deadly to life—indeed, it is often used in hospitals to sterilize equipment. Even the small amount that does pass through the atmosphere is capable of causing serious burns, as anyone who has been careless enough to stay out in the sun can testify. In moderate doses, it stimulates the production in the skin of a pigment called melanin, from Greek *melas*, black. The function of this pigment is to protect the skin from further damage due to ultraviolet radiation.

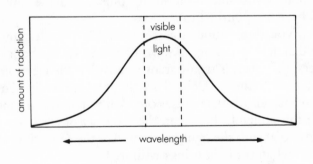

FIGURE 11.1

If the light coming through window glass fails to produce this pigment response, it must mean that the glass, like the ozone layer, screens out the ultraviolet component of sunlight even as it allows ordinary light to come through. The real issue, then, is how glass can accomplish this separation.

To understand this phenomenon, think back to our picture of electrons as bound into a complex web of forces. The stronger these forces are—the stiffer the springs—the harder it is for the incoming wave to move the electrons and the less energy the electrons can absorb. From the fact that glass is transparent to visible light, we concluded that its electrons are locked too tightly to be moved; hence, they absorb almost no energy as the wave passes by. From the fact that glass absorbs ultraviolet rays, however, we must conclude that the forces exerted by that type of radiation are strong enough to overcome the inertia of the web and transfer energy from the wave to the electrons. Once that transfer has taken place, the same processes go on that we discussed on page 126, and the wave gradually diminishes as it moves farther through the glass.

This conclusion also tells us about the web of forces in many of the substances found in nature. For example, one could argue that the most important interaction on earth that involves light is photosynthesis, the process by which plants convert the energy of incoming sunlight to the sugars that form the basis of the entire food chain on our planet. As a by-product, photosynthesis also releases the oxygen that we breathe.

The key step in this process is the absorption of incoming light by the chlorophyll molecule. Chlorophyll is a complex chain structure, as sketched in Figure 11.2; the details of the way it converts energy into food are still being worked out by biochemists. Nevertheless we can deduce something about the way this molecule works by simply using the knowledge acquired in thinking about atoms, light, and color.

In the first place, we know that most of the energy in sunlight lies in the visible band. It must be, therefore, that at least some of the electrons in the chlorophyll atom are bound loosely enough to allow them to absorb energy from visible light. It follows that the structure of chlorophyll must be different from that of glass. Second, we know that it is the presence of chlo-

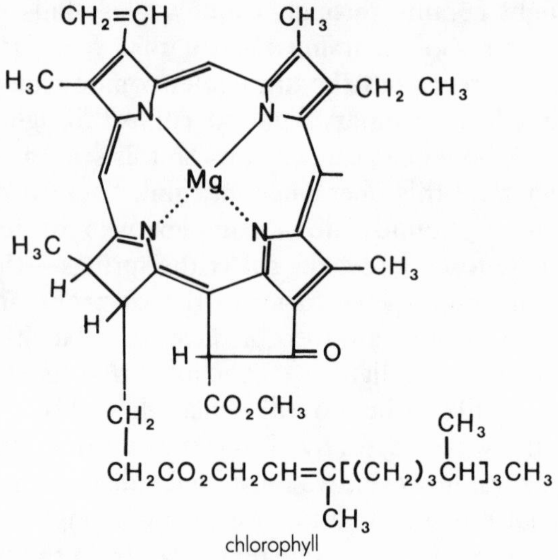

chlorophyll

FIGURE 11.2

rophyll that gives leaves and other plant parts their characteristic green color. Since we know that the color of an object is produced by light waves that penetrate into the interior and are transmitted back to the eye, we conclude that the chlorophyll molecule is not capable of absorbing the color green. When light is sent out as a secondary wave from the material in a leaf, green gets to our eye unimpeded by chlorophyll, while all other wavelengths are absorbed.

It turns out that the "working electrons" in chlorophyll—the ones that absorb the sunlight—lie either above or below the complex of atoms shown in Figure 11.2. Electrons in the plane of the molecule tend to lie close to many atoms and are therefore tightly locked in. Like their counterparts in glass, they cannot absorb visible light. Electrons above or below the plane, however, are more loosely tied to the rest of the molecule and therefore can (and do) respond to visible light and, in the process, initiate the cycle responsible for life.

With this analysis of window glass and chlorophyll, we have reached the limit of what we can do with a model of the atom that pictures the electron as attached to a spring. It is not surprising that we should reach such a limit—the model is, after all, pretty crude. What is surprising is that with its aid we have been able to understand so much. It gives us hope that nature is, in the final analysis, simple and beautiful. If it weren't, it is unlikely that we would have been able to unravel as much of the physics of color as we have.

To go further, we have to introduce the modern, quantum-mechanical picture of the atom. In this model, we imagine that the electron circles the nucleus in well-defined orbits, much as the planets circle the sun. Unlike the planets, however, the electrons can circle the nucleus only in certain specified orbits like the ones shown in Figure 11.3. In the jargon of physics, the electron orbits are *quantized*. The study of systems in which things are quantized is quantum mechanics.

If we want to move an electron from an inner orbit to one farther out, as shown, we have to exert a force to overcome the attraction of the nucleus, that is, we have to supply energy to the atom to move the electron. Conversely, if the electron moves from an outer orbit to an inner one, it gives up energy to its surroundings. The amount of energy in both cases is equal to the amount required to move the electron to the outer orbit, or, equivalently, to the difference in energy between the two orbits.

This point can be made explicit by means of a diagram such

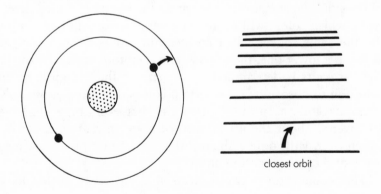

closest orbit

FIGURE 11.3

as that shown on the right in the figure. Each line in the diagram corresponds to the energy the electron has in one of its orbits. As the orbits get farther and farther away from the nucleus, the energy needed to lift an electron to them gets higher and higher, and the lines in the energy-level diagram corresponding to those orbits move farther up. By this diagram we indicate that the energy needed to move an electron from one orbit to another is the distance between the lines corresponding to those orbits. Thus, the transition between orbits shown on the left is represented by the arrow between two energy levels on the right.

One way of supplying the energy to the electron is to have it interact with light. We saw in chapter 9 that electrons can absorb energy from a light wave the way a cork can absorb energy from a water wave. But the quantum-mechanical atom presents an important difference between the electron and the cork. The electron can absorb energy only in chunks corresponding to the distances between the lines in the diagram. It cannot absorb an amount of energy that would leave it stranded between levels. In other words, a given atom can absorb only certain well-defined amounts of energy.

But the energy of a light wave depends on the wavelength. That an atom can absorb only certain energies means that it can absorb only certain colors. In other words, in the quantum-mechanical picture the discrete energy levels play the same role as did the stiffness of the spring in chapter 9—they determine which colors will be absorbed and which will pass on by. By the same token, when an electron moves from an upper orbit to a lower one, the energy (and therefore the color) of the light it emits is determined by the size of the energy gap. In addition to absorbing only certain colors, the atom emits only certain colors, as well. This means that everything we have discovered about the production of color in materials can be taken over, with only a slight difference of interpretation, into the world of the quantum atom.

This connection between electron orbits and emitted light was exploited in a branch of science called spectroscopy during the nineteenth century. You can understand the basics of this science by consulting Figure 11.4. Suppose that energy is

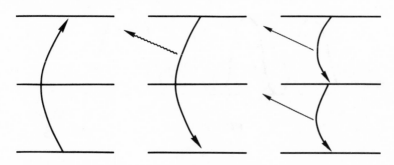

FIGURE 11.4

added to an atom so that an electron can go from the lowest energy level (corresponding to the closest orbit and called the "ground state") to the higher level shown on the left. This energy can be added to the atom by a passing light wave, of course, but it can equally well come from a collision with another atom or from other, less familiar, processes. Once the electron has been moved up, it can get back to the ground state in one of two ways. The electron can jump all the way back to the ground state, as shown in the center, or it can make two successive jumps, as shown on the right.

These two possible sequences of events give rise to different emitted light waves. The first, a single jump through a relatively large energy interval, produces a high-energy (blue) wave, while the two smaller jumps will give rise to light at lower energies (red). If we had a large collection of atoms to which energy had been added (e.g., by heating), we would expect to see both processes in action. Consequently, if we looked at the collection of atoms through a prism, we would see something like the results shown in Figure 11.5. The atoms would emit light in three colors, one for each of the possible jumps the electron can make. Which of the colors is brightest depends on the number of atoms making each jump.

Spectroscopy is, in essence, the application in reverse of the chain of reasoning we have just gone through. Instead of at-

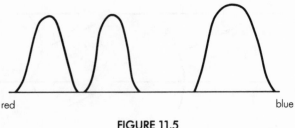

red   blue

FIGURE 11.5

tempting to deduce the nature of emitted light from the energy levels of the atom, it concerns itself with deducing the nature of the atoms from the observation of the emitted light. The task of the spectroscopist is to look at the wavelengths (Fig. 11.5) and deduce the energy levels (Fig. 11.4).

The ability to work backward in this way is very important for astronomy, where we can measure the light given off by distant objects but never get samples of those objects to analyze in the laboratory. Under those conditions, the ability to work out energy levels from light is critical, because it turns out that these energy levels are like fingerprints—they are different for each of the more than one hundred known chemical elements. Thus, by looking at the light from a star, the astronomer can tell what atoms are present there, even though the star is hundreds or even millions of light-years away. It is thanks to this analysis of light that we have discovered what sort of materials our universe is made of.

But another aspect of the energy-level diagrams is even more interesting than this one. That aspect is the scale of the energies observed in moving from one line in an energy-level diagram to another. This relates to the question I raised when I asked why one can't get a tan through a window, the question of how much energy is needed to move electrons from one orbit to another.

To grasp this problem, we must first learn to think with an unfamiliar but very convenient unit of energy—the electron volt (eV). It is defined as the amount of energy it takes to move one electron through one volt. Thus, if you pushed an electron from the outer edge of a flashlight battery to the little knob at the center, you would have to expend 1.5 eV, whereas if you moved the same electron from one pole of your car battery to the other, you would expend 12 eV.

Physicists use this unit of energy to study the structure of the atom and its constituents. They compute that the energy required to move electrons from one level to another in a typical atom is roughly 1–10 eV, or something intermediate between our examples of a flashlight and a car battery. Since it takes about this amount of energy to lift an electron up, it loses this amount when the electron falls back down. Consequently, the light that it emits also carries this amount of energy away from the atom.

If a few eV is the scale of the energy in the change within the atom that produces light, it is also the energy scale for all the changes that we call chemical reactions. This connection between chemistry and light may sound at first like a *non sequitur*. Think for a moment, though, about what a chemical reaction really is at the atomic level. Two or more atoms come near each other (see Fig. 11.6) and either share or exchange electrons, creating an electrical force that bonds them together. The atoms have formed a molecule, and a chemical reaction has occurred, but from the point of view of the atoms, what has happened? Some electrons in their outer reaches have simply been shuffled around. But this is precisely what happens when light is absorbed and emitted, although in that case the electrons are shuffled within a single atom. Once this similar-

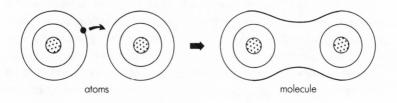

atoms   molecule

FIGURE 11.6

ity is seen, the statement that the electron volt is the energy scale for both chemistry and light seems entirely reasonable.

This interpretation of light as arising from the movement of electrons from one orbit to another also explains why it is that so many forms of radiation similar to light are found in nature. If we consider molecules instead of atoms, we find that the electrons in those molecules also have discrete energy levels whose differences are much smaller than the corresponding differences for atoms. When transitions between these states occur in molecules, radiation is emitted that has the same structure as light (see chapter 9) but with a much longer wavelength and a much lower energy. Depending on the wavelength, we may be talking about infrared radiation, microwave radiation, or radio waves. Typical wavelengths for these three may be, respectively, a few nanometers, a few centimeters, and a few miles, and the energies involved may run from a fraction of an eV to a millionth of an eV or less.*

It should be clear by now that visible light—the stuff that the eye detects—is only one member of a broad, continuous band of radiation types. Light is important to us because we have evolved on a planet where the atmosphere is largely transparent to this form of radiation and largely opaque to others; but in the grand scheme of things light does not enjoy the privileged place it occupies in our minds. It is neither the most nor the least energetic type of radiation, nor is it the most common. If you had to choose among the various types of radiation by guessing which occurs most often in the universe, you would have to pick microwaves as the champion, for in our era it is that sort of radiation that bathes and pervades the universe. It is the echo of the Big Bang that started it all.

To further understand the place of light in the universe, one must extend the picture of the origins of radiation by looking at energies above the eV range. In very heavy atoms—atoms with many electrons in orbit and a large positive charge on the nucleus—the electrons in the innermost orbits are subjected to very strong electrical forces. Consequently, the energy differ-

---

*Although we are discussing this radiation in terms of emission from atoms and molecules, remember the discussion in chapter 9, in which other ways of producing the same waves are given.

ences between orbits will be large. If a situation like the one shown in Figure 11.7 should arise, in which an electron is knocked out of an inner orbit, another electron will make the downward transition and emit radiation. This process is shown in the energy-level diagram on the right. The radiation emitted can have energies from tens to thousands of eV, depending on the atom and orbit involved. The lower end of this energy range corresponds to the ultraviolet radiation that causes sunburn, while at the upper end we are dealing with soft X rays. (The meaning of "soft" will become obvious shortly.) There is thus a smooth transition from radio waves to visible light to X rays, a transition characterized by the scale of the energies involved in the process that gives rise to the radiation.

The energy unit of a 1,000 eV, a keV or kiloelectron volt, is the measure of the energy required to move one electron across 1,000 volts or a thousand electrons across 1 V. Other units are the MeV (million electron volt) and the GeV (gigaelectron volt). The latter corresponds to a billion electron volts as the term "billion" is used in America. Indeed, the unit used to be called the BeV. But since Americans and Europeans differ in their use of billion, a change had to be made. To an American, a billion is a thousand million, whereas to a European it is a million million and what we call a billion they call a milliard. To avoid confusion, the prefix "giga," from the Greek root for

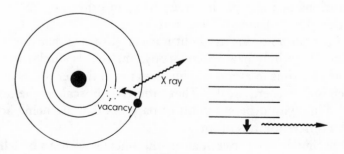

FIGURE 11.7

"giant," was adopted by international convention to replace billion.

When we get to energy scales of KeV we have reached the limits of what can be done by shuffling electrons around in atoms, even heavy atoms. But radiation in the MeV and GeV ranges actually occurs in nature. In order to find its source, one must look for systems in which the differences between energy levels are much higher than they are in the outer reaches of atoms.

Such a system exists in the nucleus. Just as electrons circle in orbits around the nucleus, the protons and neutrons inside the nucleus follow their own, more complex orbits. The particles in the nucleus are bound together by the action of the so-called strong force,* which, although it operates only at short range, is roughly a hundred times more powerful than the electrical force that operates among electrons. Consequently, the protons and neutrons are much more tightly bound into the nucleus than the electrons are in the atom. The energy scale of the nucleus is measured in MeV rather than in eV, which means that it requires a million times as much energy to move a proton as it does to move an electron. This in turn means that you must supply several MeV of energy to move protons and neutrons to new orbits or remove them from the nucleus. It also means that when protons or neutrons fall down to vacant orbits, they will give off radiation whose energy is in the MeV range. This sort of radiation is called "hard" X rays. Hospital X-ray machines typically use X rays in the 100 KeV to MeV range. In some machines these rays are generated by nuclear transitions of the type described here; in others, by the rapid deceleration of beams of electrons.

The main point for us about nuclear X rays is that they give rise to an entirely new spectroscopy, one that is similar to that of the electrons in atoms but involves much tighter orbits and a much higher energy scale. That difference in scale is the result of dealing with different kinds of particles that are being acted on by different kinds of force.

The similarities between atom and nucleus seem to be telling

---

*A discussion of the forces of nature and the hierarchy of their strengths is given in my book *The Moment of Creation* (Scribners, 1983).

us that nature possesses a limited number of patterns and that the patterns repeat in very different situations. We are reminded of the phenomenon of independent evolution, in which we see the same mechanism (e.g., large dorsal fins in dinosaurs) developing over and over again in different kinds of organisms.

The twin examples of the atom and the nucleus tell us another important fact about the nature of the subatomic world: the existence of a series of discrete emissions of the type shown in Figure 11.5 (p. 154) is the outward manifestation of a composite system. In other words, if the system emitting the radiation is such that it consists of some basic particles that can be arranged in many different ways, then when those particles are rearranged, they will emit radiation only at certain well-defined frequencies.

Understanding this connection between composite systems and discrete spectra was very important in the 1960s, when physicists were studying the short-lived elementary particles that live, along with protons and neutrons, in the nuclei of atoms.* One of the great surprises in modern science was the overwhelming number of these sorts of particles—over two hundred at last count. One of the main goals of physicists was then to find some way of bringing order into this collection.

There are two important clues that will help us to understand the chain of events that followed. The first is that the particles can be grouped in families. If we make a diagram of the masses of the particles in a given family, we get something like what is shown in Figure 11.8 (p. 160)—which is remarkably like an energy-level diagram. The second clue is contained in the equivalence of mass and energy implicit in Einstein's famous formula $E = mc^2$. This equivalence tells us that if we have enough energy, we can turn it into mass and create a particle; and conversely, if we have a particle, we can convert all or part of its mass into energy. Both aspects of the equivalence—energy into mass and mass into energy—can be seen any day in the physics laboratories and commercial nuclear reactors around the world.

---

*The story of the discovery of the elementary particles is given in my book *From Atoms to Quarks* (Scribners, 1979).

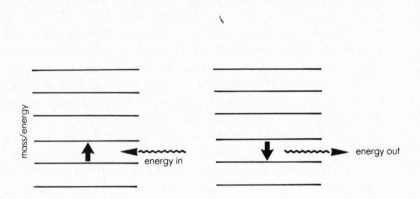

FIGURE 11.8

With these two clues in mind, let us turn back to the problem of unraveling the mystery of the elementary particles. When we make a "mass-energy" level diagram of a family of particles, as in Figure 11.8, we find that if we add energy to one member of the family (e.g., by letting it absorb energetic radiation or a smaller particle), it will be transformed into another, higher-mass member of the family as shown on the left. Conversely, if we watch a higher-mass member of the family for a while, it will spontaneously emit energy in the form of radiation or of another particle and will be transformed into a lower-mass member of the family, as shown on the right. There is a one-to-one correspondence between the properties of the mass-energy diagram for elementary particles and the energy-level diagrams that we constructed for atoms and nuclei.

The primary difference between the atomic, nuclear, and particle spectroscopies is the energy involved in each. The scale of the atom is measured in eV, the scale of the nucleus in MeV, and the scale of the particles in GeV. Radiation in the GeV range—the stuff that corresponds to X rays in nuclei—is called the gamma ray. Once again, we find nature repeating a familiar pattern in a new situation.

The connection between composite structure and spectroscopy also enables us to understand another development in physics. Just as the energy levels of the atom arise from rearrangements of electrons and the energy levels of the nucleus arise from the rearrangement of protons and neutrons, we can attribute the mass-energy levels of particle families to the rearrangement of a new species of fundamental entities called quarks. According to current theories, all of the two hundred or more elementary particles that have been discovered are nothing more than different arrangements of six types of quarks. At the moment, there is a good deal of indirect evidence for the existence of quarks, but none has been seen in the laboratory.

Most physicists believe that with the discovery of quarks we have come to the end of the road—that the three spectroscopies are all there is in nature. A small group of less conventionally minded scientists, however, has begun to ask whether we might not find nature repeating its now familiar pattern at a still deeper and more energetic level. If they turn out to be right, we will eventually discover a spectroscopy of quarks and conclude that they are made of things more elementary still. Perhaps there is no end to this sequence. Perhaps as our ability to probe deeper increases, we shall find not three or four but a never-ending infinity of spectroscopies awaiting us, each one the spitting image of the one that keeps us from getting a suntan through a window.

TWELVE

Lightning Bolts
and Life

N O ONE CAN WATCH the sky very long without seeing lightning. Although probably no atmospheric phenomenon has been more misunderstood or maligned than lightning, as we shall see, it may well be that no life would be found on earth (and hence no one to produce colorful folktales) if lightning did not exist.

The presence of lightning in the sky also teaches us something very important about our atmosphere. So far, we have discussed atmospheric properties in terms of phase changes, clouds, the transmission of light, and other processes in which the air plays a more or less passive role. Lightning shows that in addition to these occurrences, there are important electrical effects present in the atmosphere—effects that go far beyond the lightning stroke itself.

My own introduction to the electrical nature of lightning

came one summer evening in Virginia. I was sitting in my living room reading when there was a sudden bright flash followed by a thunderclap so loud that it knocked some pictures off the wall. The next morning, when I went to take a shower, I discovered there was no water in the house—the lightning stroke had burned up my water pump. I was puzzled, because the pump was at the bottom of a 150-foot well, but in talking to my neighbors, I found that this sort of thing was quite common in the country. Partly out of curiosity, partly to find some way to prevent a recurrence, and partly to see if I could sell an article to a magazine and recoup some of the cost of replacing the pump, I started looking into the phenomenon of lightning. What I found was fascinating.

Almost every cultural tradition has a rich folklore about lightning. The Indians of the southwestern part of North America saw it as a snake traveling from the heavens to the earth. In the East, other Indians believed that the flash represented the wing feathers of the thunderbird, and they attributed lightning damage to the bird's claws. A similar legend exists among African tribes, with the addition that the thunderbird left eggs on the earth that had magical powers of healing.

Some scholars believe that the legend of Prometheus, the fire bringer, originated with the observation of lightning. According to that Greek legend, you will recall, Prometheus, one of the immortal Titans, took pity on humankind and stole fire from the Gods and brought it to earth. As punishment, he was doomed to be chained to a rock and have an eagle eat a piece of his liver each day, which renewed itself by night. He was eventually freed by Hercules. There is a very good chance that the original fires captured by primitive men were started by lightning strokes in the forest. Such events are actually fairly common—about two-thirds of forest fires in the United States are started by lightning, and on a single day (July 12, 1940) lightning started no fewer than 335 fires in the western United States.

The folklore about how to avoid lightning strokes is as diverse as it is wrong. In the Ozark Mountains, for example, it is thought that hiding scissors will protect you from lightning.

Fire festivals in medieval Europe were supposed to protect villages from lightning, and our own Fourth of July fireworks are probably descended from these festivals. Perhaps the most interesting lightning-prevention scheme was that used in the medieval cathedrals. These buildings, with their tall steeples towering over everything in the countryside, served as natural targets for lightning. It was believed that ringing the cathedral bells during an electric storm would keep the building safe, and many bells had the phrase *Fulgura Frango* ("I break up the lightning") cast into their sides. So many bell ringers were killed trying to ward off the bolts that the practice was finally outlawed.

The connection between lightning and fire is an obvious one and can readily be verified by simple observation. The connection between lightning and electricity is less obvious. It was the American statesman, author, and amateur scientist Benjamin Franklin who made this connection as part of his study of the nature of electricity. Most people are surprised to find that Franklin, revered as one of the Founding Fathers, made important contributions to basic science, but it's fair to say that he would be remembered for his work as an early "electrician" even if he had never been near the Declaration of Independence.

Franklin was the first to realize that all electrical effects could be understood in terms of the flow of a single "electrical fluid" in and out of objects. In modern terminology, he recognized that it is the electrons that move, while the positively charged nuclei of atoms tend to remain fixed. In the course of his studies, he built a number of machines to help generate electricity. You can reproduce the working principle of these machines yourself. On the next dry day, run a comb through your hair and then bring it near some bits of paper. The paper will stick to the comb—an effect called static electricity. When an object like the comb is rubbed against something else, such as your hair, electrons are scraped off one object and added to the other. (Which direction they take depends on the details of the material's structure.) The result: a comb that either has too many electrons, and therefore has a negative electrical charge, or has too few and is thus positive.

The law that governs the force between electrical charges is simple: like charges repel, unlike charges attract, and the force becomes smaller as the distance between the charges increases. Suppose for the sake of argument that we bring a negatively charged object near a piece of paper. The electrons in the paper, being free to move, will be pushed away from the object by the repulsive electrical force. This leaves behind a region of the paper with a net positive charge, and the force between this region and the original charged object will be attractive. It is a process like this that causes the paper to stick to the comb on a dry day. The same forces operate to cause sheets of paper coming out of a copying machine to stick together and causes certain kinds of clothing to cling in dry weather.

What caused Franklin to make the connection between bits of paper sticking to a comb and lightning is something you can also see for yourself. Have you ever had the experience of walking across a rug and then feeling a little shock in your hand when you reach for a doorknob? Next time you're in this situation, take a key out of your pocket and touch the doorknob with it. You'll see a small spark jump from the key to the metal knob. If you listen carefully, you'll hear a little "crack" as the spark jumps.

What happened is that in rubbing your feet on the rug, you have built up an electrical charge. Under the influence of forces like those described above, this charge jumps across to the doorknob, creating the spark and the sound. Franklin built a machine that generated a constant supply of static electricity by working a crank to turn a bottle against a piece of buckskin and noted the spark discharge. He observed, as you can, that this discharge is something very much like a lightning bolt in miniature. This suggested to him that lightning might be a large-scale version of what he could produce in his laboratory. He verified this conjecture by flying a kite during a Philadelphia thunderstorm, observing sparks jumping from a metal key attached to the kite string. This experiment led Franklin to the invention of the lightning rod, a subject we'll consider in more detail in the next chapter.

Once we understand that lightning is electrical in nature, we can begin to talk about how it is produced. The breeding ground of the lightning bolt is the dark, towering cumulo-nimbus cloud. These clouds, well known as harbingers of the storm, may stretch from altitudes of 5,000 feet to as much as 40,000 feet. Inside such a cloud, it is not at all unusual for the temperature to change by as much as 100° between the top and the bottom, so that it can be hailing within the upper reaches of the cloud and raining at the lower. As you might expect in such a chaotic system, there are all sorts of turbulent air currents within the cloud. This turbulence causes collisions to occur between the various types of particles in the cloud. Just as running the comb through your hair causes the comb to pick up an electrical charge, repeated collisions in the thundercloud cause materials to become charged, either positively or negatively. We aren't really sure of the details of what happens next, but we do know that the lighter particles in the cloud usually tend to pick up a negative charge, while the heavier ones become positive. The updrafts of air inside the cloud have an easier time lifting the light, positive particles to the top. Consequently, the positive and negative electrical charge within the cloud separates, with the lower layers usually being negative and the upper parts positive (see Fig. 12.1). Since the upper part of the cumulonimbus cloud is generally many thousands of feet higher than the bottom layer, the positive charge will have relatively little influence on someone on the ground. Consequently, from here on we can ignore it and treat the cloud as having only a negatively charged layer at its bottom.

The negative charges in the cloud will then exert force on opposite charges in the ground beneath. If, as is always the case, there are loose electrons wandering around in this area, they will be pushed away as shown. Similarly, if there are atoms in the neighborhood that have lost electrons and therefore have a net positive electrical charge, they will be attracted to the area under the cloud. Atoms of this type, with a deficit of electrons, are called ions.

The result of all of this electrical interplay is that there will be an area on the ground—called the image—roughly the same shape as the cloud, an area that has a positive electrical charge and will follow beneath the cloud as it moves along. The layer of air between the image and the cloud prevents the positive and negative charges from coming together, but the

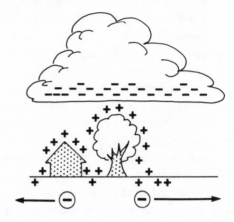

FIGURE 12.1

attractive forces are still there, and the two sets of charges move along in lockstep as the wind carries the cloud through the air. If there should be some sort of obstacle on the ground —a hill or a tall tree—the charges in the image will run up one side of it and down the other, always trying to reach the cloud overhead. The electrical currents in this sort of movement are small but can easily be measured in trees and buildings.

I was once told an interesting story by the late Jesse Beams. Beams was one of the great experimental physicists of his generation and played a major role in the Manhattan Project during World War II. He told me about a time before the war when a group of physicists had driven out into the high desert with a vanload of electronic equipment to make some measurements of atmospheric electricity. During the day the clouds started to build up, and suddenly all the instruments began to go haywire. Realizing that they were seeing the effects of the image charge, the physicists all raced for the metal van. No sooner had the last one got to safety inside than what appeared to be the world's largest lightning stroke hit a tree outside, frying their electronics in the process. Sensitive instruments and some basic knowledge of electricity probably saved a few lives that day.

Some anecdotes report that people have felt the hair on their necks stand up just before a lightning stroke—an effect attributed to the flow of the image charge. I am a little skeptical of these claims because the currents are generally too weak to be felt. I could be wrong, of course—it wouldn't be the first time. Nevertheless, I wouldn't recommend relying on this sort of symptom for an early warning of lightning.

The ominous black thundercloud, then, is to be thought of as a lightning bolt waiting to happen. The opposite charges in the cloud and the ground exert attractions on each other. There is enough charge involved in this situation to produce the massive flow of electrical energy we associate with lightning; all that is needed is some mechanism to allow the two charges to penetrate the intervening gap of air.

Under normal circumstances, air is an example of what is called an insulator—a material through which electrical current cannot move. Other examples of insulators are glass, ceramics, and plastics. The reason such materials do not carry current is that all of the electrons in them are tightly bound to their individual atoms and none are free to move. Figure 12.2 shows a typical atom in the atmosphere, with its full complement of electrons. Under normal circumstances, the electrons

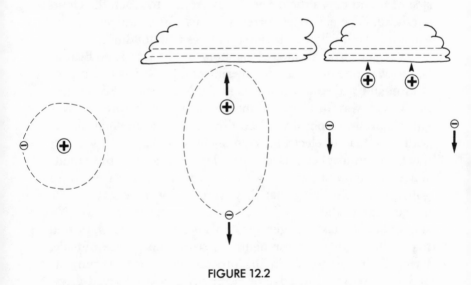

FIGURE 12.2

would simply circle the nucleus forever. But if this atom happens to be circulating in the air near the bottom layer of a thundercloud, the situation changes. The large negative electrical charge in the cloud tends to repel the electron and attract the nucleus, as shown in the middle of Figure 12.2. In effect, the cloud tries to tear the atom apart. If there is a large enough charge in the cloud, the electron will indeed be torn loose, as shown on the right. The result is that the air beneath the cloud is transformed from a material with no loose electrons to one in which there are many free electrons and ions. Such a material, called a plasma, is a very good conductor of electricity. The thundercloud is thus capable of tearing its own conducting path through the air, a path that will allow the cloud and image charges to come together.

For years it was thought that this is what caused lightning—that the charge was too big for the layer of air to handle, so the air broke down and a lightning bolt struck. But high-speed cameras have now demonstrated that something much more complex occurs. The charge above builds up and punches out a tunnel of ionized material several hundred feet long in the air underneath (see Fig. 12.3). This conduction tunnel is called a "leader," through which the negative charge in the cloud is free to flow down. Once this has happened, another leader is punched out, lower down: the charge gets closer to the ground with each successive step. The process is similar to driving a nail; it's much easier to hammer it in with a succession of light blows than to pound it in all at once.

There will usually be a dozen or more leaders in a given chain. As the leaders descend from the cloud, the charge from the image punches a shorter leader up from the ground, and the two meet about a hundred feet above the earth, opening a conducting pathway between the image charge and the cloud. Suddenly the image charge runs up into the cloud, thereby neutralizing the negative charge. This flow is called the "return stroke," but it is perceived as a lightning bolt. The entire process from first leader to stroke takes but a few thousandths of a second.

The leader mechanism is what gives the lightning stroke its crooked appearance. Each change of direction in the stroke

FIGURE 12.3

corresponds to a point at which one leader gives out and another starts. Sometimes two leaders branch out from a point and two channels are opened. Then, as the image charge runs up both paths into the cloud, what we see is forked lightning.

This mechanism explains many phenomena observable in the sky, for example, the "heat lightning" often seen on hot summer evenings. It looks like broad flashes of light, usually along the horizon, and it is almost never accompanied by rain. Heat lightning is actually a normal stroke in reverse. Instead of opening a conducting path to the ground, the charges at the bottom of the cloud punch open a series of leaders inside the cloud itself. The tunnel formed unites the positive charges at the top with the negative ones on the bottom, and the resulting flash lights up the whole cloud from the inside. If this happens to a cloud high in the sky, it is sometimes called sheet lightning.

Our understanding of charge movement should dispel what is perhaps the most widespread misapprehension about lightning—that it never strikes twice in the same place. It is obvious that the leader mechanism will be more efficient in punching through thin layers of air than through thick ones. As the image charge moves along the ground, it decreases the thickness of the air layer every time it climbs an obstacle. A tall tree, for example, may shorten by a hundred feet the path that has to be opened. Consequently, as the cloud approaches, a situation can easily develop in which the charge is not strong enough to punch through the normal air layer but is sufficient to get through to the top of the tall tree. In this case, the tree will be hit by a lightning stroke.

The tree is a victim because of the geometry of the insulating layer of air between image charge and cloud charge. If this causes the tree to be struck once, it is obvious that the tree is likely to be struck again. Lightning not only strikes more than once in the same place; it is also more *likely* to strike where it has already struck than it is to strike somewhere else. The Empire State Building in New York, for example, has been hit hundreds of times since it was built.

Knowing that lightning is actually an electrical current also explains some of the things that happen when it strikes. As the very name leaders reminds us, electrical current flows most easily along paths of conducting material. Now, ordinary water is a pretty good conductor of electricity, and lightning often follows trails of moisture. For example, if lightning hits a tree, it will probably run down to the ground through the moist layer just beneath the bark. When so much energy flows through such a layer, it generates a lot of heat. The water is converted to steam, and the bark literally explodes. The result is a long jagged tear down the side of the tree—a tear the Indians attributed to the claws of the firebird. You can probably see such trees next time you're in the woods.

That lightning is an electrical current also explains how it was able to burn out my pump, 150 feet underground. The pump is connected to the surface by electrical wires that form a continuous circuit that goes all the way back to the house and, eventually, to the generating station. If a large electrical current such as that which causes a stroke of lightning flows near a circuit of wires, an effect known as induction occurs, that is, a current flows in the circuit. Consequently, when lightning strikes near power lines it induces a surge of current that is then free to travel along those lines. These surges have been known to travel down power lines and follow them into a house, where they burn out appliances like freezers or refrigerators; they can even cause fires. My surge probably started in the wires going out to the pump and followed them down the well to the motor windings. Good-bye, pump!

Induction also explains another event experienced by mountain climbers who run into thunderstorms. These climbers often crawl into small caves or overhangs to protect themselves and are knocked unconscious when lightning strikes nearby. In this case, the induction occurs in the delicate circuitry of the human nervous system and, although seldom fatal, can cause some rather unpleasant effects.

Fully 15 percent of the several hundred lightning deaths that occur in the United States each year happen to people who have sought shelter from the rain under a tall tree. From our discussion, it is easy to see that such behavior is the most dangerous thing you can do during a thunderstorm.

There is a simple commonsense rule that will lower the risk of being struck by lightning during a storm—avoid being the tallest thing around or even being near the tallest thing. Many lightning deaths occur in open areas such as golf courses or swimming pools because the human being standing upright there is the tallest target available to the stroke. In such a place, the best thing to do is get out of the danger zone as quickly as possible.

Another point, illustrated by the story of the physicists in the desert, is that lightning will follow the easiest conducting path to the ground. Consequently, if you're in a car or a building, your best bet is to stay there. Even if lightning hits your car, it will run through the metal skin and follow the wet tires to the ground, leaving you safe.

No discussion of lightning would be complete without a comment on the thunder that accompanies the stroke. When an electrical discharge passes through air, a cylinder of air around the stroke is rapidly heated and begins to expand. (This occurs both for the leaders and the return stroke, but there is so much more energy in the return stroke that we can forget about leaders when we consider the genesis of thunder.) So sudden is the heating, in fact, that for the first few feet of its path, the expanding air actually moves at supersonic speeds. This expanding envelope of air pushes on the still air of the atmosphere, creating a sound wave in much the same way as a moving diaphragm in a speaker creates a sound wave in your stereo. The sound created in this way, after it has traveled through the air to our ears, is what we hear as thunder.

This explanation of the phenomenon explains a number of facts. First, the path of a lightning stroke is usually very long. The sound wave emanates from each different part of the stroke, so that it doesn't reach our ears all at once. This explains why we perceive the thunder as lasting for an extended period—a series of booms and rumbles instead of a single crash. This also explains the old Boy Scout method of estimating how far away a thunderbolt is. This method, you may recall, is to count the number of seconds between the time you see the lightning and the time you hear the thunder and divide by five. The result gives you the distance to the bolt in thousands of feet.

This method works because while the transmission of light through the atmosphere is, for all intents and purposes, instantaneous, sound travels at the leisurely rate of (approximately) one thousand feet per second. The counting procedure, then, is a way of measuring the time it takes sound to travel from its source. I use this method all the time around my home, because (just to play it safe) I like to disconnect my water well when there's a lightning storm within a mile of the place. One burned-out pump is enough!

As we explore the intricate anatomy of an individual lightning bolt, it is easy to lose sight of the fact that lightning bolts, taken as a whole, are a significant source of energy in the earth's atmosphere. At any given moment, there are roughly two thousand thunderstorms going on at various places on the earth, each capable of producing lightning bolts. In some areas, such as Uganda, they are almost daily occurrences; in others, such as the Pacific Coast of the United States, they are rare. On the average, however, some eight to nine million lightning bolts strike the earth every twenty-four hours.

The ubiquitous nature of lightning may have been important in the development of life when the earth was young. At that time the atmosphere was composed of gases very different from those present today. The most likely constituents were methane (natural gas), carbon dioxide, water vapor, hydrogen, and ammonia. The present atmosphere, composed primarily of nitrogen and oxygen, is largely due to the effects of living organisms and is only a few billion years old. Those living organisms themselves formed relatively quickly after the earth was created. The oldest fossils of single-celled organisms date back 3.8 billion years, while the earth itself is about 4.5 billion years old.*

Sometime during the first eight hundred million years of the planet's existence, then, something happened to turn the raw materials of the earth's atmosphere, rocks, and oceans into something we would grace with the title "living things." The first step in the process leading to life would have been chemical evolution—that is, the transmutation of available chemicals into the long organic molecules that are the components of ail life. It is in this first step in evolution that lightning may have played an important role.

For various reasons, it is believed that organic molecules first formed in the earth's atmosphere and then rained down on the oceans, transforming them into a thin soup of organic materials. We are not certain how life developed from the soup, but we have a pretty good notion of how its basic organic molecules came to be formed in the first place.

In order to form complex molecules from simple ones, we must have some source of energy to drive the reactions. Other than sunlight itself, the largest source of energy in the atmosphere of the early earth was lightning. It delivered 50 percent more energy than radioactive decay (which was much more intense then than it is now), and three hundred times as much as volcanic eruptions (which were also more common then). In addition, lightning, as we saw, delivered its energy over the entire earth, whereas volcanoes would produce intense heating in a localized area. Consequently, when scientists first began to think about the origins of life, it was to lightning as a source of energy that their thoughts turned.

In 1953, two scientists at the University of Chicago—Harold Urey and Stanley Miller—set up an experimental apparatus

---

*Bob Rood and I, in our book *Are We Alone?* (Scribners, 1981), give a detailed discussion of the formation of life on earth and the possibility of the same events happening elsewhere in the galaxy.

like the one shown in Figure 12.4. Urey and Miller filled a bulb with gases thought to be present in the earth's early atmosphere and subjected it to electrical sparks to simulate the effects of lightning. They boiled water in another bulb and allowed the vapor to circulate through the system to simulate the natural movements of gases. Any organic molecules that formed were trapped in the liquid water, where they remained until chemical analysis could be performed.

With this simple apparatus, Urey and Miller hoped to reproduce whatever chemical reactions took place in the atmosphere of the primitive earth. As the experiment ran for a few weeks, they saw the water in the trap begin to turn a murky brown color. When they analyzed the fluid, they found it contained many simple organic compounds up to and including amino acids, which are the basic constituents of proteins and other

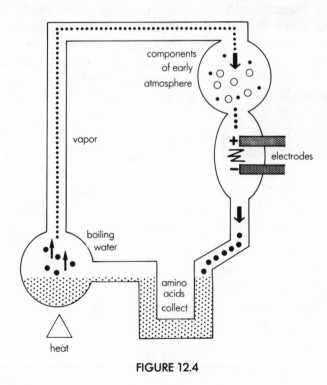

FIGURE 12.4

more complex molecules essential to life. Figure 12.5 shows sketches of the molecules present in the early atmosphere and glycine, a typical amino acid. Obviously, what the electrical discharge did was to provide enough energy to the system to allow the various atoms to rearrange themselves into more complex forms.

Since 1953, the study of the origins of life has become much more sophisticated, and we now know of thousands of complex molecules that can be formed in this sort of experiment. We also know that not only electrical discharge but ultraviolet radiation and even heat can serve as energy sources for such reactions. Our picture of the early earth, then, is one in which these complex molecules formed in the atmosphere and entered the oceans in a sort of biological rain. Simple calculations show that we would expect amino acids to be produced at the rate of about one ton per second—a rate high enough so that after a "mere" hundred million years, the ocean would be a 1 percent broth of organic material. (You can compare this with the 3 percent concentration of salt in the present ocean.)

Once this broth forms, we reach a gap in our knowledge of the evolution of life. There are many theories about how the primeval soup turned itself into the first reproducing cell, but

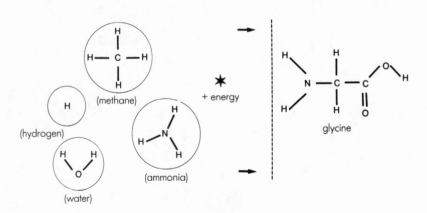

FIGURE 12.5

all we know for certain is that by the time the fossil record starts, some six hundred million years later, primitive one-celled organisms had appeared. From that point on, chemical evolution was replaced by natural selection as the driving force of life, and a few billion years later sentient, self-aware life in the form of human beings appeared.

So the next time you see a lightning bolt, remember that although it can clearly threaten life, it is also true that without those bolts there might not have been any life on earth at all.

THIRTEEN

Lightning Rods and the Research Pipeline

B ENJAMIN FRANKLIN, practical man that he was, was not content merely to come to a theoretical understanding of lightning. He immediately turned this knowledge to use, inventing a device—the lightning rod—that has since protected mankind from the scourge of the lightning bolt. In 1753, he published an article in his *Poor Richard's Almanac* entitled "How to secure Houses etc. from LIGHTNING." I know of no better way to introduce the lightning rod than to use Franklin's own words.

It has pleased God in his goodness to Mankind, at length to discover to them the Means of securing their Habitations and other Buildings from Mischief by Thunder and Lightning. The Method is this: Provide a small Iron Rod (it may be made of the Rod-iron used by the Nailers) but of such a Length, that one End being three or four Feet in the moist Ground, the other may be six or eight Feet above the highest Part of the Building. To the upper End of the Rod fasten a Foot of Brass Wire the Size of a common Knitting-needle, sharpened to a fine Point; the Rod may be secured to the House by a few small Staples. If the House or Barn be long, there may be a Rod and Point at each End, and a middling Wire along the Ridge from one to the other. A House thus furnished will not be damaged by Lightning, it being attracted by the Points, and passing thro the Metal into the Ground without hurting any Thing. Vessels also, having a sharp pointed rod fix'd on the Top of their Masts, with a Wire from the Foot of the Rod reaching down, round one of the Shrouds, to the Water, will not be hurt by Lightning.

With our understanding of the mechanism of lightning bolts, we can see how the lightning rod works. When the image charge comes to a house equipped as Franklin described, it runs up to the top of the house, but it also runs up the iron rod. Since the rod is taller than the house, it is closer to the bottom of the cloud. Consequently, when the leaders start to form, they will move toward the charge on the rod rather than the charge on the house. When the conducting path is finally opened, the charges in the image can move directly from the earth through the iron rod and into the cloud. The electrical charges are neutralized in a way that does not threaten the structure of the house.

In fact, since Franklin's time we have learned a lot about the basic principles that make his invention work. The general principle involved is that electrical current, like water, will always flow along the path of least resistance. To the thundercloud, the iron lightning rod represents a sort of superhighway. The house is also a possible conducting path but resembles an overgrown and rocky logging road. Given the choice, the current takes the superhighway every time.

We must realize that it is the total path traversed—air plus lightning rod—that determines the resistance to the passage of electrical current. A cloud charge at position *A* in Figure 13.1, for example, will find the air path to be little different for a strike through the house and one through the lightning rod. It is only in the second half of the two paths, where one runs through the house and the other through the rod, that a difference becomes manifest. The lower resistance of the rod therefore comes into play and draws the stroke.

But for a cloud in position B, the situation is not so clear. In order to reach the lightning rod, the cloud charge has to open a much longer path through the air than to the house. The question of whether the relative difficulty of reaching the rod is compensated for by the smooth path to ground once the rod is reached depends on the particulars of the situation. The cloud charge, in fact, is confronted by the same sort of choice as often confronts hikers. Is it better to scramble up a steep hillside to reach the relatively smooth going in the field at the top, or is it better to angle up along the side of the hill, taking a path that is easier than the hillside but harder than the meadow?

Engineers have developed a rule of thumb for dealing with this kind of question. The geometry around a lightning rod is such that everything inside a cone whose radius is equal to the height of the rod will be protected by it. This so-called cone of protection is shown in Figure 13.1. In that figure, the top of

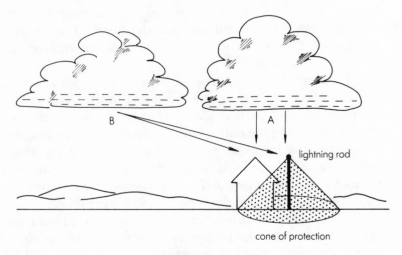

FIGURE 13.1

the house sticks up above the cone, so it is susceptible to lightning strikes. Had the rod been taller or closer to the house, the protection would have been complete.

The principle of a cone of protection explains something that North American farmers knew long before Franklin's invention. If a house is built in an area with frequent lightning storms, it will be relatively safe if there are tall trees near the house. As we saw in chapter 12, a tree provides a path for lightning and can therefore act as a natural lightning rod, drawing the bolts away from houses within their cones of protection. Of course, there are dangers in using trees for this purpose, the obvious one being that the lightning will cause all or part of the tree to fall on the house. Nevertheless, before Franklin's invention this bit of folk wisdom probably saved quite a few lives.

This theoretical understanding of how the lightning rod works was not possessed by Franklin's contemporaries, because even after the discovery of the electrical nature of lightning there was much to learn about its operation. Franklin installed a lightning rod on his house in Philadelphia but ran the metal inside the house into an apparatus that consisted of two brass bells, about 6 inches apart, with a brass ball suspended between them. One bell was connected to the end of the lightning rod on the roof, the other to the end of the rod going to the ground. When lightning struck, the apparatus acted like a doorbell—the brass ball swung back and forth between the bells, ringing them and letting Franklin know that there was electricity running through. Franklin used this gadget to tell him when electricity was in the clouds so that he could study it. The presence of the apparatus in his study must have worried his wife—understandably, I think. In 1758, when he was in London, he wrote to her that if the bells bothered her she could connect them with a metal wire so that the wire "will conduct the lightning without ringing or snapping, but silently."

The lack of exact understanding about lightning led to a great deal of controversy in Europe. The battle over the adoption of the new device was fought on many fronts, some philosophical, some political, and some petty and personal. At the time—the late eighteenth century—the widespread use of gunpowder by the military made the issue of lightning protection particularly important. In 1767, for example, the authorities in Venice decided that it was sacrilegious to suggest that God would cause lightning to strike a church and so stored hundreds of tons of powder in a church vault. When the inevitable happened, three thousand people were killed, and an entire section of the town was destroyed. Perhaps this event, along with the detonation of a powder magazine in Brescia in 1772, explains why Italy became a leader in adopting Franklin's invention. Within a decade such famous landmarks as the Cathedral of San Marco in Venice and St. Peter's in Rome had been fitted with lightning rods.

Elsewhere acceptance came more slowly. In England, the then current dispute with America led to a tempest in a teapot when a member of a Royal Commission (which included Franklin) argued that the pointed rods would "unnecessarily invite lightning strokes" and recommended blunt ends on the rods. Today we know this detail is of little importance, but because of the political animus, the controversy got blown all out of proportion in the press. Franklin, displaying the wisdom for which he is so justly famed, refused to get caught up in the debate, and eventually it died down.

In France, events took a more serious turn. The Abbé Nollet had opposed Franklin on some point of interpretation in early electrical experiments and, as sometimes happens even among scientists today, took a personal dislike to Franklin and made it his business to oppose him on everything, including lightning rods. So great was his influence among his countrymen that their old belief about churches being exempt from lightning strikes persisted. On April 14, 1781, a terrible lightning storm moved across Brittany, striking no fewer than twenty-four churches. One church was destroyed, all sustained some damage, and two bell ringers were killed trying to avert the strokes. After that, the French started to construct rods according to Franklin's prescription.

As time went by, more and more anecdotal evidence accumulated in favor of the efficacy of Franklin's device. In Batavia harbor, in what was then the Dutch East Indies, lightning struck two ships anchored side by side. One, British, was fitted with a lightning rod and remained unharmed. The other, a Dutch man-of-war, was destroyed.

In Siena, crowds gathered in the Piazza on April 18, 1777. The great tower there had been equipped with a lightning rod, over the strenuous objections of some prominent members of the aristocracy. On this particular afternoon, a storm was clearly imminent. Curiosity seekers filled the square to see if the lightning rod would work and were rewarded with a spectacular strike, complete with the smell of sulphur. The tower survived unscathed. By the end of the century, events like these had convinced the skeptical, and the lightning rod was in wide use on both sides of the Atlantic.

What is one to make of this disjointed set of events? On the one hand, you might look at the displays of stubborn bigotry, petty personalities, and general ignorance that followed the introduction of the lightning rod, and despair of our race. On the other hand, it was only about forty years from the time that Franklin first published his results to the time when the lightning rod was in widespread use. This fact strikes me as hopeful: given enough evidence (and hard experience), people are capable of change.

The story of the adoption of the lightning rod illustrates an important point about the way that new devices and techniques enter everyday life. It may be true that if you build a better mousetrap the world will beat a path to your door, but the world may take its own sweet time doing it. Many an aspiring inventor has gone bankrupt waiting for his work to be adopted. In our own day, when inventions and innovations seem to be coming down the road at breakneck pace, we can learn by looking at what happened in the past.

Much as engineers may deplore it, the truth is that the resistance to a new device (or its adoption) involves deep human emotions. The process is subject to all the vagaries and downright cussedness that humans display in every part of their lives. Simple rationality plays a role, of course, but it is not the only thing that does. The lightning rod aroused every kind of feeling—religious, political, personal—and proper skepticism, too: some worried lest the new device invite lightning and cause the evil it was meant to avert. Such motives are not in themselves reprehensible; they account for the normal human tendency to conserve previous knowledge and be wary of change.

Nor is the inability to recognize a major technical achievement confined to "early days" by any means. In his marvelous work about the Bell Telephone Laboratories *Three Degrees Above Zero* (Scribners, 1984), Jeremy Bernstein discusses the advent of the transistor, the device that is the backbone of our modern electronics industry. He points out that it was fully four years between the time the existence of the device was announced and the time it was used in the telephone system and five years before it appeared in a salable device (a hearing aid). The first transistor radio cost the equivalent of more than two hundred dollars in today's money, and it was not exactly a commercial success. Someone evaluating the transistor in the early 1950s could certainly be excused if he failed to recognize its potential for transforming our society. Even the august *New York Times* ran Bell Lab's announcement about the development of the transistor below an article about a new quiz show called "On Your Mark."

When I think about the obstacles faced by innovative technology, I am reminded of a business lunch I attended recently. I was with a prominent publisher, a literate man who writes poetry on the side, and a colleague who is one of the nation's leading experts on literary criticism. My companions quickly launched into comparisons of their home computer systems, matching wits about kilobytes, RAM, and all the rest of the lingo. After a while, they turned to me and asked me what I wrote on. I replied "a Remington portable" (the same battered old typewriter I'm using now). Then, in a display of oneupmanship that only a physicist could pull off in that sort of situation, I added: "I don't process words; I write them."

But after lunch I began to think about the exchange. After all, as a physicist-author, I would seem to be a prime candidate for a word-processor salesman. Perhaps my own motives in resisting their blandishments illustrate the point I made above about human cussedness.

Not that I'm afraid of computers; I started programming them as an undergraduate (in machine language, no less). I have a terminal in my office that connects me to a huge Control Data number cruncher, and I routinely write codes running to many thousands of lines to carry out calculations in my research. To me, working with a computer is like driving a car—I neither enjoy it nor hate it; and I am ready to use it to get a job finished.

When word processors first came out, I argued that they were too expensive. Now that I can no longer do that, I have to discover and confess my real reason for avoiding them. The reason is that I like to have a suntan. On warm autumn or spring weekends, I take my old Remington out into the fields surrounding my house, strip to the waist, and write in the sunlight. I do the same in Montana during the summers, where I have the added benefit of spectacular views of the Rocky Mountains. Until recently, using a word processor would have made this outdoor exercise impossible, because they weren't portable. Is this reason for resisting a new technology any less or any more silly than those adduced for not installing lightning rods? I think not.

The spread of inventions in society at large, then, depends as much on social and psychological factors as it does on physics. But if we turn our attention from acceptance to invention, we find that the development of the lightning rod is typical of the way original ideas are transformed into useful products. We can use the development of the lightning rod to understand how insights go from being "science" to being "technology."

Understanding this link is particularly important today if for no other reason than that we have become extremely dependent on applied science in our everyday lives. I like to think of the path a strange new idea in a university laboratory must travel if it is to become a nuts-and-bolts product on a manufacturer's shelf as a pipeline. One end of the pipe is the rarefied atmosphere of the basic research laboratory; the other end is the marketplace. We can trace this pipeline by looking at how Franklin got interested in electricity and lightning in the first place.

In 1743, Franklin saw in a lecture given by one Archibald Spencer in Boston a demonstration of some electrical phenomena. He was intrigued by what he saw but did nothing about it until 1746, a year after a Fellow of the Royal Society in London donated some electrical apparatus to the Library Company of Philadelphia, of which Franklin was the founder. In Franklin's words: "[I] eagerly seized the Opportunity of repeating what I had seen in Boston, and by much Practice acquired great Readiness in performing those also which we had an account of from England, adding a number of new Ones."

From reading Franklin's autobiography, it is clear that he was like a kid with a new toy. In addition to devising a number of ingenious devices to supply himself with "electrical fluid," he analyzed the "Leyden jar" (a piece of early electrical apparatus) and showed that electrical charges resided in solid bodies, not in wires or the atmosphere. Since electricity was a new subject for study in those days, Franklin had no immediate urge to find practical uses for his discoveries. He pursued the subject for the sheer joy of adding to the store of human knowledge. He did not think his experiments would lead him to discover a way of diverting lightning bolts; he was just curious about how electricity worked. This is the characteristic of the scientist involved in what is usually termed "basic" research—research conducted not for utility or monetary reward but for the acquisition of knowledge. The appellation "basic" is used to distinguish this type of research from "applied research," which aims at a practical outcome rather than knowledge alone.

My own experience has led me to believe that this simple division of research into basic and applied is oversimplified. I have taken part in several large-scale projects for applying science—some in medicine, some in nuclear engineering—and I have come to the conclusion that there are at least four different types of scientific work that get done as something moves down the pipeline from basic research to a useful product or commercial application. All these steps are illustrated in the story of the lightning rod.

Basic research is certainly the field in which new scientific ideas are born. It is the type of research we associate with university scientists. The reward system for scientists carrying out basic research is in one respect strange—rewards are based almost entirely on the judgment of one's peers. The gain from a well-done piece of basic research is usually not monetary but consists of increased respect from other basic researchers. The sum total of the reputation of its members is what constitutes the reputation of a university department of science or major laboratory.

What is the sort of thing that enhances the reputation of a basic researcher? His goal is to add to the store of knowledge about the world regardless of whether the new knowledge is useful or not. In any field there is always a consensus as to what constitutes the major problems to be solved. For example, in high-energy physics today, the chief problems have to do with the development of unified field theories.* In other branches of science the problems are different, but a consensus exists as to what they are. Research work is judged according to how much it contributes to the solution of the major problems. Work that does not make such a contribution is seldom condemned: it is simply ignored.

Again, in the sciences, there is no particular prejudice *against* usefulness in the results attained by basic research—it is simply irrelevant. The development of the laser, for example, has had widespread applications in areas from surgery to mining, but it was motivated by an attempt to understand the behavior of atoms, and the enormous prestige that accrued to its developers came from the fact that it shed light on basic atomic processes. Franklin's studies of electricity, up to and including his discovery of the electrical nature of lightning, would be classified as basic research. He was motivated by curiosity alone.

Since in the short term it is difficult to show a payoff from basic research, it is done primarily at universities and large government laboratories, where immediate utility is less important than long-term gains. There are a few corporate exceptions to this general rule, Bell Telephone Laboratories being the most notable.

The next step in the movement of an idea from basic research to the marketplace is what I call the *acquisition of basic knowledge*. This is research aimed at understanding basic physical processes, and in that regard it resembles basic re-

---

*The discussion of these theories is given in my book *The Moment of Creation* (Scribners, 1983).

search. But it is motivated by a desire to produce a useful result. For example, after Franklin's discovery of the nature of lightning, there followed a lot of research into the area he had opened up. Some of this was ongoing research in electricity, but some was directed at a fuller understanding of lightning so that better lightning rods could be built. It is this type of research that falls into the acquisition-of-basic-knowledge category. Much of the current flowering of research into the electronic properties of solids is research of this type. The microelectronics industry provides a constant impetus for the development of new kinds of solids, with electronic properties that can be used in the bewildering variety of new devices.

Writers on this topic often maintain that the only difference between basic and applied research is in the motive of the scientist and not in the work itself. Although I agree that the dividing line between basic research and the acquisition of basic knowledge is not sharp (what dividing line is?), I think that much more goes into its definition than the purpose in the mind of the researcher. Having worked in both areas myself, I know that it is not just the state of mind that differs but the work itself. A great difference comes from the focus in what is done and what is left undone. For example, if you develop a mathematical model in basic research, you will explore all the implications of the model just to see what happens. But if you develop a similar model while pursuing the acquisition of basic knowledge, you are almost certain to restrict your exploration to those aspects of the model that apply to your particular problem. If, for instance, you're designing an airplane wing, you will study the airflow only for speeds likely to be reached by the plane. You really don't want to know anything about the supersonic flight characteristics of a small private propeller plane. In these and other conditions, the way the problem is posed affects the questions that are asked and answered and thus what work is done and not done.

Because the acquisition of basic knowledge has a short-term payoff, it is often performed in industrial research laboratories. It also constitutes some (but not all) of the work done in engineering departments of universities and large government laboratories.

The next step in the pipeline is *applied research*. This research concentrates on a specified practical problem but one that still retains some measure of generality. For example, work on the question whether a pointed or a blunt lightning rod is better, or the question whether the pointed rod "invited" lightning strokes, was applied research—research aimed at the very narrow application of knowledge to produce an improved lightning rod. Yet any results obtained would be useful to anyone making lightning rods, so the research retains an element of the universality attached to both basic research and the acquisition of basic knowledge. Because it is immensely practical, applied research is normally done in industrial laboratories and only occasionally in the universities.

Finally, we come to *development.* In this phase of work, the general principles that have been discovered are applied to a specific problem. The men who designed the lightning-protection system for St. Peter's in Rome, for example, were dealing with only one demand—to protect that cathedral from lightning. To accomplish their purpose, however, they had to use the knowledge that had been gained in each of the three previous stages of research. Similarly, the engineers and scientists who designed and built the space shuttle for the aerospace companies were engaged in development. Development is almost always carried out in an industrial or commercial setting.

In these days, it seems that the governor of every state in the union is trying to promote "research" so as to develop local versions of high-tech centers like Silicon Valley in California. In making policy, though, it's a good idea to remember that not all research is likely to lead to increases in the tax base. Only the last two phases of the pipeline are directly linked to the sort of manufacturing industries that our leaders have in mind when they talk about "research" or "R & D."

As the example of the lightning rod shows, without the ideas feeding in from basic research, the whole research-and-development enterprise would soon dry up. How far would the papal engineer have got in protecting the magnificent dome at St. Peter's if Benjamin Franklin had not been curious about electricity? By the same token, how far do you suppose the Silicon Valley geniuses would get in designing new miniaturized electronics today if a group of ivory-tower university physicists in the 1920s and 1930s had not devoted their lives to uncovering the secret of the behavior of atoms? Each step in the progression, from the seemingly impractical work of the basic researcher to the nuts-and-bolts decisions of the engineer developing a product, is indispensable. In a very obvious sense, our entire technological civilization depends on each step being carried out in sequence.

Unfortunately, that basic research acts as the beginning of the pipeline means that it is a very tempting target for budget cuts. Moreover, the effects of cutting back this type of research take a long time to be felt, because the pipeline is at the moment full. The example of the lightning rod shows that reducing the flow of basic research is a shortsighted policy that beggars future generations for small savings today. Fortunately, the federal government, which supports almost all the basic research in the country, has so far taken the farsighted view of the importance of basic research.

Whenever I am asked why millions (or billions) of dollars must be spent on ever-larger particle accelerators and new adventures in space, I point out that our current high-tech boom is the result of past generations putting new knowledge into the research pipeline, knowledge that is now being used to better the human condition. I would, in fact, be hard put to think of any major development in science that has not paid off manifold by the time it has made its way through the pipeline. The Apollo program, which put a man on the moon in 1969, was once the favorite whipping boy of those who felt that that kind of "progress" was a pointless endeavor. Yet today half of the long-distance phone calls in the United States go through orbiting communications satellites, and we routinely use weather satellites to save billions in property and thousands of lives by giving early warnings of storms. That item in the pipeline is paying off with a vengeance.

The truth is, when we have to decide whether to support basic research, we are in the position of someone who has to decide whether to bet on a horse that has paid off 100-to-1 every time it has run in the past. There is no guarantee that it will do it the next time, of course, but you'd be a fool not to put your money on it again.

FOURTEEN

Ball Lightning, UFOs, and Other Strange Things in the Sky

T HE LIGHTNING BOLT is surely the most dramatic, as well as the most common, phenomenon associated with atmospheric electricity. But it is far from being the only electrical display in the sky. Some of the others, like St. Elmo's fire and ball lightning, are every bit as fascinating as ordinary lightning. Of additional interest is that if we ask how scientists feel about rare and ill-understood phenomena, we can get an idea of the wavering boundary between science and pseudoscience. This boundary has always attracted people interested in the scientific enterprise. Why are some subjects, such as the study of unidentified flying objects (UFOs), considered to be outside the pale, while others, on the face of things equally bizarre, are given the official stamp of approval? How is the line between these subjects drawn? Who decides what is respectable and what isn't? The only way to answer this sort of question is to look closely at subject areas that fall barely within the territory on each side of the line.

One characteristic most of these borderline subjects share is that they are relatively rare and transient phenomena. Their rarity makes it difficult for scientists to study them. Two electrical displays—St. Elmo's fire and ball lightning—are good examples of the effect that frequency of occurrence has on scientific judgment. Both are rare, but ball lightning is especially so. Consequently, until quite recently ball lightning was often classified as pseudoscience and put on the wrong side of the line. This fate was never suffered by St. Elmo's fire.

St. Elmo is the name of a fourth-century Italian bishop. The name is actually a corruption of Erasmus, which was probably the bishop's real name. Elmo was supposed to have been martyred during the persecution of Christians under the Emperor Diocletian. For some reason, he became associated with an electrical display often seen by sailors and now called St. Elmo's fire. It is a cool, crackling, greenish discharge around the masts and spars of ships at sea. Unlike lightning, St. Elmo's fire does not damage the material it touches. Sailors took it as evidence that the saint was nearby, watching over them. Thus, St. Elmo became one of the patron saints of sailors and "those at peril on the sea."

Legend has it that during Ferdinand Magellan's historic voyage around the globe in the early sixteenth century, his crews became discouraged with the constant storms and unknown waters. They were apparently on the verge of insisting that the ships return to Portugal when one of the sailors saw St. Elmo's fire on the mast. Soon after, the storms abated; the sailors took it as a sign that St. Elmo was still with them even though they were in waters no Christian had ever sailed. They took heart and finished the first circumnavigation of the globe.

Sailors are not the only ones to encounter St. Elmo's fire. Mountain climbers often see green halos around their ice axes, and Swiss peasants have reported that when their cattle are taken to high pasture in the summer, they often display "flaming horns." Numerous reports of the green fire clinging to trees and high towers have also been common from the Middle Ages on.

Because of all this anecdotal evidence, the existence of St. Elmo's fire was never really doubted. It has always, like lightning itself, been a legitimate object of scientific study. Today we believe it is a subclass of the phenomenon often encountered in the operation of high-voltage systems, called corona discharge. It works this way: in chapter 12 we saw that the presence of large collections of electrical charges distorted and sometimes tore apart atoms in the air. This is what leads to the formation of leaders and eventually to the lightning stroke. This process can take place near the image charge on the ground or near the thundercloud. If a large positive charge has flowed up a tree or the mast of a ship and is trying to get at the negative charge in the cloud, it is quite possible that a large volume of air will be ionized. The electrons that have been torn from the atoms will be pulled toward the mast or tree. In that process they heat up the air and cause it to glow. In effect, the positive-image charge creates a natural version of the fluorescent bulb. We believe that this is what we perceive as St. Elmo's fire.

The salient features of St. Elmo's fire as a subject, then, are these: it was reported so often that it could not be ignored, and there were explanations for it that fitted well into existing ideas about the workings of electricity. No unheard of effects had to be invoked to explain it, so scientists do not have to depart from the company of any of their cherished beliefs to deal with it.

The situation with ball lightning is somewhat different. It is a much rarer phenomenon, and reports are few and far between. When it is seen (almost always after a lightning stroke), it consists of a luminous sphere between 6 inches or a foot across, but occasionally as large as 2 feet. It glows about as brightly as fluorescent light and can be of any color. It normally moves around, sometimes following electrical conductors like telephone and power lines. It can endure for anything from a few seconds to a few minutes, and it leaves evidence of its passage in the form of charred wood or burned-out wires.

There is plenty of folklore about ball lightning—stories of the glowing sphere coming down chimneys, running across a room, and escaping out a window, for example. In the western United States, it was the custom to supply Forest Service watchtowers with tall, metal-legged stools. The explanation I was given was that the stools were so designed that when ball lightning came in it would run around the legs of the stool, trying to get at the ranger, but get discouraged and go out the window. The existence of such folktales played some role in the skepticism with which scientists viewed the whole phenomenon.

The real obstacle wasn't the folklore but the fact that so few trained scientific observers had seen ball lightning. In the nineteenth century, moreover, there was no convenient theoretical niche into which something like ball lightning could be placed. Given the absence of absolutely incontrovertible evidence for its existence, the consensus among scientists was that it could be safely ignored.

The situation changed with the advent of modern atomic physics. The new understanding of the plasma state of matter —the state in which electrons have been stripped from atoms and float freely in incandescent materials—led to the realization that there was nothing inherently improbable about ball lightning. In addition, the construction of laboratories in places like Los Alamos, New Mexico, led to large numbers of scientists living out in the country away from the cities. Thus a lot of high-powered minds had a look at unfamiliar phenomena in nature. One such individual, the late Berndt Mathias of the University of California at La Jolla, adopted ball lightning as his hobby.

Mathias used to set up a camera, point it at approaching thunderstorms, and open the shutter for several minutes. Any lightning activity from the storm would be recorded on the film. I remember a visit he made to the University of Virginia shortly before his untimely death. He gave the usual formal talk on his research specialty (the fabrication of new materials with unusual electrical properties) but insisted on leading an informal brown-bag lunch seminar on ball lightning. After going through a long discussion of the history and physics of the phenomenon, he showed one of his slides. It showed a streak of orange light, something like an auto headlight in a time-exposure photograph. The light appeared near a tall tower, then jumped down to the ground and ran along some wires until it left the frame. This photo, along with a few others, is the only photograph I have ever seen that stands a good chance of being a record of ball lightning. I have to point out, though, that this photograph can be explained in other ways. Ordinary lightning strokes, for example, are known to follow wires and jump through air gaps.

Despite the lack of clear evidence for the existence of ball lightning, by 1955 the eminent Soviet theoretical physicist Peter Kapitza (since awarded the Nobel Prize for other work) put forward a theory to explain the phenomenon. In 1963, the journal *Scientific American*, which is about as close to the mainstream of scientific thought as it is possible to get, ran an article (complete with a photo from Mathias) that summarized the attempts to explain how ball lightning might occur. Clearly, by the postwar years, ball lightning had become a fit subject for scientific investigation. No comprehensive theory had been developed: indeed, none exists even today. Nevertheless, a scientist would not be held in contempt by his peers if he decided to work on the problem.

Having said this, I should point out that the question of whether there is any photographic evidence for ball lightning is still open. In 1973 the Swiss meteorologist Klaus Berger, the veteran of more than thirty years of lightning studies, published a review in the prestigious German journal *Naturwissenschaften* in which he asserted that there is no photograph in existence that proves the existence of ball lightning. He cited evidence that some photographs taken in the 1930s were actually fireworks set off by practical jokers to fool a physicist and that another famous photograph (showing a glowing ball with streamers) was actually an electrical transformer that had been hit by ordinary lightning. A strong current of skepticism thus persists in the scientific community about the existence of ball lightning. On the whole scientists have adopted a "show me" attitude and remain unconvinced that a case has been made. Still, members of this group would agree that the study of the question is a legitimate scientific enterprise.

Suppose you were set the task of explaining the phenomenon of ball lightning. How would you proceed? If you were a physicist, it's very likely that you would set out to determine the scale of energy involved in the ball. This would give you some idea of the sort of processes that would have to be involved in creating it. If you assume that the ball is made up of atoms that have lost one electron each, then a straightforward calculation shows that the total energy locked up in a ball 10 inches in diameter is about 18 cents' worth of electrical energy at the price charged nowadays by public utilities in the United States. It is also about the food value (200 calories) of a large slice of cake or two small glasses of wine. This is a respectable amount of energy but not one that is so large as to be difficult to find in nature. It is only a tiny fraction, for example, of the energy involved in a single lightning stroke.

Oddly enough, there is one eyewitness account that tends to back up this estimate of the energy in ball lightning. On October 3, 1936, the London *Daily Mail* reported that a ball was seen to cut through some telephone wires, come through an open window (leaving scorch marks behind), and dive into a barrel of water. The water, estimated at 4 gallons, proceeded to boil. If we believe this account and work out the energy needed to boil 4 gallons of water we may estimate the energy content of the ball at roughly four times that given above. We seem to be in the right ballpark.

Unfortunately, this line of thought takes us only a small distance. One of the objections to believing that ball lightning is some sort of plasma of electrons and ions is that in the open air such a system is very unstable. Electrical forces operate to bring the electrons and the ions back together again, and calculations would indicate an expected lifetime for the ball of a few hundredths of a second. That the balls can last for minutes suggests that the real problem to be solved is not how to account for the energy needed to create the ball but to find a way to explain the ball's continuing existence once it has been formed.

Basically, there are two classes of theories to explain the creation and maintenance of the ball. In one class, a way is found that would pump energy into the ball from the outside. In the other class, the ball is constructed in such a way that enough energy is stored or generated internally to overcome the tendency of the charges to recombine.

Kapitza's original theory was of the former type. He assumed that an originating lightning bolt would set up a series of electromagnetic waves, something on the order of water waves sloshing around in a bathtub. In this model, the electrical charges created by ionization tend to collect at the troughs of waves, like debris on the surface of boiling water. The field itself can create new ions as the old ones recombine, so that the plasma is continuously replenished. In this scheme, all the energy comes from the original lightning bolt.

But there are two difficulties (fatal ones, I think) with the theory. First, no one has detected the sort of electromagnetic waves needed for the theory to work in actual lightning strokes. Second, if you take the *Daily Mail* event seriously, you have to conclude that the ball contains enough energy to boil water, even if it is cut off from contact with outside sources of energy. To believe the wave theory, you have to discount the story in the newspaper—not a terribly hard thing to do.

The second class of theories assumes that the original lightning bolt stores enough energy in the ball at the moment it is formed to keep things perking along. A typical theory holds that the ball is actually a species of miniature thundercloud. The original stroke somehow produces oppositely charged regions from bits of material, such as dust motes, that are normally in the air. The millions of tiny lightning strokes that neutralize these charges are what is seen as the glow of the ball lightning. Although this scheme explains how a ball could live a relatively long time, it gives no explanation of why a lightning bolt should produce a neatly segregated set of charged particles in the first place.

More recently, some theorists have suggested that ball lightning might even be a miniature nuclear reactor, isolated from the environment by electrical effects. These theories, generally proposed by those who are familiar with plasmas because they work in the field of thermonuclear fusion, remain highly speculative.

The status of ball lightning, then, remains somewhat unsatisfactory. We accept that it occurs, albeit rarely, and we have some general ideas about what causes it. But we lack a satisfactory theory to explain it.

What lessons can we draw from St. Elmo's fire and ball lightning? First we learn that anecdotal accounts of sightings are enough to convince scientists that there is something to be taken seriously, particularly if those sightings can be explained in terms of a general theoretical framework. Second, we see that it is not at all necessary to have a satisfactory theoretical explanation of something in order for it to be considered worthy of study. There is still no good theory that explains ball lightning, but no scientist risks the scorn of his fellows if he studies it. What follows, then, is that there are two separate questions that must be asked and answered when we have to decide on which side of the line between science and pseudoscience a particular subject is to be placed. We have to ask whether there really is something to be studied, and if so, whether we have a theoretical framework into which the phenomenon may fit. Only the first question matters when it comes to discussing pseudoscience. As the example of ball lightning shows, the lack of theoretical understanding is no bar to the acceptance of a particular subject as legitimate for scientific study.

Having said this, I hasten to add that the decision is not totally independent of theory. As with so much of science, we are faced here with the necessity of making a judgment based on many factors. In the case of ball lightning, the lack of copious sightings was certainly a major stumbling block to acceptance, but so was the early nineteenth-century lack of knowledge about atomic structure and plasmas. I suspect that the transfer of ball lightning across the dividing line, though due in large part to new and more reliable eyewitness accounts, was also influenced by a better understanding of the way that atoms and electricity interact. In the late nineteenth century one of the major fields of research involved the study of electrical discharges of gases in vacuum tubes. No one who spent his time working with such phenomena could doubt that strange things can happen when electricity and atoms mix. Furthermore, there is a natural progression from ordinary lightning to St. Elmo's fire to ball lightning. They go from common to rare, but we can detect a kinship among them. Once all are recognized as electrical effects, ball lightning gains legitimacy from its association with its commoner brothers.

As we remarked earlier, most scientists would place the study of UFOs firmly on the far side of the science-pseudo-science boundary. Yet there are some resemblances between UFOs and ball lightning. Both, for example, place great emphasis on eyewitness accounts of phenomena. Ball lightning is often cited by UFOlogists as an example of the closed mind of the scientific community and as a justification for carrying on their studies.

In order to meet the charge that I, too, may not be open-minded enough to give UFOs a fair chance, let me digress for a moment and tell you a little about some of my recent professional activity. Several years ago, I was a founding member (and later vice-president) of an organization known as the Society for Scientific Exploration. The two hundred members were primarily academic scholars, and there was only one guiding principle for the group: no question would be considered too far out to be discussed at meetings, provided that the most rigorous scholarly standards were applied. In other words, the society was to provide a forum in which serious work on subjects normally beyond the pale could be presented and listened to by open-minded peers. Reincarnation, after-death experience, the Loch Ness monster, and, of course, UFOs, were among the things that came up at our meetings. Consequently, when I say that there is no validity to the analogy between UFOs and ball lightning, I do not say so because of a closed mind but because of the knowledge I acquired by hearing (and arguing with) the best scientists who are trying to legitimize the field.

The analogy claimed between UFOs and ball lightning breaks down first in the number of sightings involved. Ball lightning is truly rare, and only a few candidates for genuine photographs exist. Since the Second World War, on the other hand, UFOs have been reported at the rate of two or three a day in the United States. If legitimacy depended only on numbers, the existence of UFOs would have been established beyond the shadow of a doubt.

In a way, the abundance of sightings of UFOs is itself a difficulty, because, as even the most ardent aficionado will tell you, over 95 percent of these sightings can be explained by conventional and rather prosaic means. The champion UFO, for example, is the planet Venus. Weather balloons, airplanes, and various kinds of optical and atmospheric effects have been reported as UFOs, and most of these can be readily identified by experienced field investigators. The real UFO question is this: after all the prosaic explanations have been given and after all the dross has been weeded out, are there really any sightings that have no conventional explanation?

In this game there are certain implicit rules about what qualifies as an "explanation." For example, a fair number of psychologists and neurologists have proposed explanations of UFO sightings in terms that most UFOlogists don't like. I recall one presentation, for example, in which a Canadian scientist presented extensive statistical correlations between UFO sightings and earthquakes. His thesis was that the changes in terrestrial electrical fields that are known to accompany geologic activity may have some sort of effect on the human nervous system, and this effect manifests itself in UFO sightings. This is a particularly intriguing idea, for if such events do actually cause sightings, no external stimulus will ever be found by investigators. Other scientists have suggested other sorts of psychoneurological explanations of UFOs.

Ingenious as this idea is, it is generally rejected out of hand by most people working in the field. They usually want to find some external physical explanation of the sightings—some explanation that must lead to an important and hitherto unknown part of science. One popular explanation (but by no means the only one) is the extraterrestrial hypothesis (ETH). This hypothesis, exploited to the point of parody in the tabloids, holds that the sightings actually involve spacecraft piloted by beings from another, more advanced, civilization. One commonly heard argument is that UFO sightings are rejected by the scientific community because scientists are not ready to accept the existence of extraterrestrials.

Actually, this argument is totally wrong. The search for extraterrestrial intelligence (SETI) has been a legitimate field of radio astronomy ever since 1959, when Phillip Morrison and Giuseppe Cocconi published a paper showing that the new radio telescopes could be used to eavesdrop on interstellar communication in our galaxy. Today, a number of very prominent astronomers are associated with the SETI program, and NASA is funding instrumentation research in the field at the rate of a few million dollars a year. These are not the characteristics of any field held to be illegitimate by the scientific establishment.

The point of this review is to show that the theoretical framework for the ETH already exists within the scientific community. The rejection of UFOs, then, does not hinge on a prejudice against the ETH. The search for the reasons why UFOs are put on the wrong side of the boundary, then, must concentrate on the first of the two questions above—is there really a phenomenon to be explained? At the psychological and social level, the answer to this question is yes—people do see strange things in the sky. I don't know of any scientist who disputes this statement. The question within the question is whether what people see is ever caused by phenomena that cannot be explained by invoking phenomena already known. It is the failure to convince the scientific community on this point that has led to the labeling of the study of UFOs as pseudoscience.

There are actually two points to the question: are there really events that cannot be explained, and second, do we see these events more often than we should on the basis of chance? As far as the first part goes, I can only give my own opinion. I have yet to see a UFO sighting for which all alternate explanations can be ruled out. A typical situation is that the data are such that you cannot rule out UFOs and the ETH, but you can't rule out a large number of other, more mundane effects, either. So long as these alternative explanations are rational, you cannot claim that you have something that needs to be explained. Let me give you a typical example. A pilot in a single-engine plane takes off from a coastal airstrip and heads for an island a hundred miles away. Halfway through the trip he starts losing altitude. A garbled voice transmission is heard (a call for help), and a strange noise comes over the radio. The plane crashes and is lost at sea. Investigators find that they cannot explain or reproduce the sound that came over the radio during the call for help.

Could this be the result of an attack by a UFO? Certainly it could, but it could also be any one of a number of things, including pilot illness or electrical trouble in the plane. The key point is that the burden of proof is on the UFOlogist—he has to prove that the existence of UFOs is the only possible way of explaining the facts. All anyone else has to do to neutralize his argument is to find a set of events that could have happened. So long as one such scenario exists, no claim can be made that there is something to be explained about UFOs.

My experience has been that even in examining the strongest UFO cases (a class that definitely does not include the example above), the burden of proof has never been met. Consequently, we can say that there is not a single UFO sighting that is not susceptible to conventional explanations.

The second part of the question—whether there are more UFO sightings than one would expect on the basis of chance—has been largely ignored by workers in the field. In chapter 4, we saw that the failure to consider the role of chance in observations destroyed the early attempts to correlate the sunspot cycle with weather. In just the same way, the appearance of one or two unexplainable UFO sightings would be significant only if it could be shown that this number was much higher than one would expect to see by chance. Even in such a mundane inquiry as the investigation of traffic accidents, there are always a few for which a cause simply cannot be found. No one claims they are due to extraterrestrial influence—our failure to pinpoint the cause is simply just taken as an example of the general cussedness of nature. In the same way, there are going to be some UFO sightings that remain unexplained no matter what.

So the case with UFOs is almost diametrically opposite to that of ball lightning. There were many sightings of ball lightning for which no other reasonable explanation existed but no theoretical framework into which to fit them. With UFOs, on the other hand, the theoretical framework exists, but there is no hard evidence of sightings. This explains why UFOs are outside the pale of legitimate science and ball lightning is inside.

This does not mean, of course, that UFOs will always be on the wrong side of the line. If tomorrow a fleet of flying saucers appeared over a major city and was seen and photographed by hundreds of people, the existence of a phenomenon to be explained would be firmly established. But until that happens, workers in the field are making a big mistake in ignoring the psychoneurological analyses of UFOs and in insisting on some variation of the extraterrestrial hypothesis. They make it much more difficult for other scientists to take them seriously. It's almost as if those who first wanted to study St. Elmo's fire had insisted that the fire really showed the presence of the saint and rejected any attempt at explanation by means of electrical discharges.

Index

ABOUT THE AUTHOR

JAMES TREFIL is a professor of physics at George Mason University in Fairfax, Virginia, and a fellow of the American Physical Society. He is also an officer and founding member of the Society for Scientific Exploration and the author of two physics textbooks and more than a hundred articles for professional journals. Winner of the AAAS-Westinghouse Award for science writing, he has been a regular contributor to *Smithsonian* and *Science Digest*. His other books include the highly acclaimed *The Moment of Creation, From Atoms to Quarks, The Unexpected Vista, Are We Alone?, Meditations at 10,000 Feet,* and *A Scientist at the Seashore*. He lives near the Blue Ridge Mountains in Virginia.